Who's At The Centre
Of Your Marriage...

The Pill or Jesus Christ?

Imprimatur **+** Noel Treanor Bishop of Down & Connor, Ireland
14th Jan. 2009

Nihil obstat   Rev. Alphonsus Cullinan D.D.

An Imprimatur and Nihil Obstat are verification that a book is free from moral or doctrinal error. They do not necessarily constitute a personal endorsement of book contents.

McCrystal, Patrick
        Who's at the Centre of Your Marriage...
            The Pill or Jesus Christ?

ISBN: 978-0-9560000-0-2

1st printing March 2009

Cover design by Guadalupe Bosco House
Photo credits William Smyth and Paul MacAree

Bible quotations from *The Holy Bible*, New International Version © 1973, 1978, 1984 by International Bible Society; Used with permission of Hodder and Stoughton Publishers. Also *Good News Bible* Catholic 2nd edition 1994 published by The Bible Societies / Harper Collins Publishers UK © American Bible Society 1966, 1971, 1976,1992. Also *New Revised Standard Version*; Catholic Edition © 1989 by the Division of Christian Education of the National Council of Churches of Christ in the USA; All rights reserved. All quotations in this book used with permission where contactable. Proper attrition missing will be gladly addressed where necessary.

Note: While the 'pill' is mentioned in the title of this book, for brevity's sake this title refers to all types of contraception used. These include sterilisation, depot injections, intra-uterine devices, sub-dermal implants, withdrawal and barrier methods of contraception.

Published by Human Life International (Ireland)
6 Belvedere Place, Dublin 1, Ireland
Tel +353 1 855 2504   Fax +353 1 855 2767
Email mail@hliireland.ie   www.hliireland.ie

More information by the author at www.dangersofcontraception.com

Who's at the Centre of Your Marriage...

The Pill or Jesus Christ?

Contraception's Disintegrating Effect on Marital Harmony

Patrick McCrystal

This work is dedicated to my
hero of the Third Millennium
Pope John Paul II,
that great Defender of the Family

and

to my wife Therese – who represents for
me the beauty and privilege of a wife open to life and
love – and who encouraged
and sustained me in the struggles and challenges
entailed in the writing of this book.

Thank you to my father and mother
for their irreplaceable role in my
being the man I am today.

Contents

Part One

The Beauty of Marriage, Family and Sexuality

Part Two

Contraception

Part Three
The Way to a Better Marriage

Appendices

Foreword

I have known Patrick McCrystal for several years, and nobody is better qualified to write a book on the subject of marital fidelity to the teachings of the Roman Catholic Church.

As a pharmacist in 1993, Patrick faced a decision that many conscientious pharmacists have faced before and since: dispense abortifacient drugs or leave the profession.

Patrick left his post, much to the surprise of his employers, and sought employment elsewhere. He was disappointed to find that nobody would employ a pharmacist with such pro-life views - not even in Catholic Ireland.

Patrick soon found that God was leading him to battle what John Paul II termed the "Culture of Death" in Ireland. He served as Director of Human Life International's Ireland branch from 1997 to 2004.

His wife Therese is also a talented speaker and witness. Together they promote the Culture of Life by the example of their family, which now includes four beautiful children (and four gone to God by miscarriage).

The timing of Patrick's book could not be better. This is the fortieth anniversary year of Pope Paul VI's great and prophetic encyclical *Humanae Vitae*. We have seen the terrible damage wrought by contraception, not only to families, but to nations and entire continents as well. Europe is hurtling down the road to total Godlessness faster and faster.

Patrick's book: *Who's at the Centre of Your Marriage ... The Pill or Jesus Christ?* seeks to play its part in rebuilding family and society in the only way possible - with Christ and the teachings of his Church as the central focus.

Early in his book, Patrick asks the question: "Do you want a marriage that you know will hold together as long as you live?" For those who answer a resounding "YES!," he spends the rest of the book outlining how such a marriage may be built.

A vital key to a happy marriage is avoiding the life-preventing act of contracepting. This is not mere theology or opinion; it is provable fact.

Patrick demonstrates why this is so in his book, which extols the natural beauty of marriage, family and sexuality. If engaged couples would read what Patrick has to say and take it all to heart, they would enjoy long and happy marriages

Maintaining a faithful and fruitful marriage is extremely difficult in the world today, and God's graces are absolutely essential if a marriage is to last. Those who voluntarily give up these graces by practicing contraception often find their marriages floundering, and they don't even know why!

A happy and enduring marriage is greatly assisted by what Patrick calls the "Seven Key Principles of Responsible Parenthood." These seven principles are a concise summary of what the Church teaches about how to live a holy and sacramental married life. They are not difficult to attain if couples have recourse to God's grace in their lives, but are virtually impossible to achieve if the couple is using contraception.

Yes, it is fortunate indeed that this useful book is being released during the fortieth anniversary year of *Humanae Vitae*. It condenses into a very readable form the essentials of the Church's eternal teachings on marriage and human sexuality, and would be especially useful in any pre-marriage course.

I strongly recommend that those couples who wish to establish a holy, happy and healthy marriage from the first day read this book from cover to cover – and then read it again and again throughout their marriages.

Fr Thomas Euteneur
President
Human Life International
Virginia, USA

Acknowledgements

I thank all those who have given practical help, editorial help, proof reading, content input, the donors of Human Life International (Ireland), the directors and staff of HLI (Ireland) and a multitude of friends who have encouraged, exhorted me and prayed for this book.

A special mention to Gerard and Marie, Tom and Mary, John and Annette, John and Liz and Emmet and Elaine - married couples who frankly and honestly shared their stories in this book.

I thank Dr Owen Gallagher, Dr Frank Dennehy, Robbie Hurley, John Lacken, Monsignor Ignacio Barreiro, Jackie Ascough, Caitriona Lynch, Bobby Forrest, Kirsten Pedersen, Dr Brian Clowes, Edel McDonough, Jameson Taylor, Paul MacAree, Fr Gerard Garrett, Bill Smyth, Des Sloyne (RIP) and my wife Therese for their insightful comments. I also want to thank John Smeaton, Selena Ewing, John Wilks, Clodagh Dunne, Marion O'Shea, Justine Donnelly, Phil Buckley, Pat Brandon, John and Meg Doherty, Jeremy and Caroline Hubert, Terry and Ann Marie McNeill and Brendan and Ann Cassidy, Neal and Teresa Doherty for their practical help and support.

To Thomas and Donna, for the invaluable gift of a quiet house and computer to write this book – thank you so much for your love and patience.

Preface

By Thérèse McCrystal

There is one comment that drives me mad. It is the common complaint "just who does the Church think it is to get into the bedroom of married couples and dictate what they should do regarding children?" or words to that effect.

Well, firstly I offer the correction that the Church never dictates, she proposes. And secondly 'she' is not an 'it'. She is a Mother. The Church has been given the task, by Christ, to help raise and guide the children of God through their life's journey on earth. She has been doing it faithfully for nearly two thousand years. It is up to us whether we embrace her wisdom or not. And indeed that is what it is, wisdom. A commodity, a process, a virtue, call it what you will, that is sadly lacking in our society today. How many people do you know who you can truthfully describe as 'wise'?

When I consider 'my options' as they are so often called, the range of advice available to me, regarding the health-care choices for my marriage, I know who I'll choose. Not the family planning centres trying to get me free from the 'entanglements' they suggest children to be; not the governments who think I don't understand anything about anything so they'll decide for me; not the pharmaceutical companies who want to make money out of me; and certainly not the media (especially dreadful radio shows who try to sound so knowledgeable and are not).

I'll go with the Mother who cares for me, who cares for my soul, who has the wisdom and experience of guiding billions of souls. On a lot of issues I've tried it my way and it does not work. She does know best. She cares the most. Most guys in the local pharmacies aren't that concerned about how I am as a person. They act as if my fertility were a sickness that needs a pill.

My husband has written this book because he has walked away from being the guy in the pharmacy handing out the pills to being a faithful son of the Church who really cares. He cares. I care. Do you?

Introduction

To those who are married - or hope to get married - do you want a marriage full of joy, a marriage that is faithful, full of love, intimacy, trust, tenderness and respect?

Do you want to still feel crazy about your spouse in one, two, five, ten, thirty or more years - to see that 'sparkle', that 'look' in your beloved's eyes for YOU? Do you want a marriage so fulfilling that you and your spouse don't even think about 'looking elsewhere', a marriage that you know will hold together as long as you live? Do you want to truly trust your spouse, to be free, to tell him or her everything?

I know a few marriages that I would wish mine to be like. A couple who are in tune with themselves and with God are a joy to be with. There is an ease, a respect, a peace in their home. You sense an order and a contentment, a clarity of their mutual and interwoven roles.

The love they have for each other is characterised by a remarkable self-giving. There is no competition or bickering. Everyone's view is valued. Differences of opinion are discussed frankly and openly. Their commitment to one another is real, human, dignified, faithful and exclusive. There is fun and laughter. Their children are cherished and esteemed and the children's joy is tangible, contagious and liberating.

This book is not a counselling book. It does not outline a comprehensive 10 step programme for a better, more intimate marriage. It does, however, lay out the evidence to show that you ABSOLUTELY NEED to avoid contraception if you wish to maximise your chances of a joy-filled marriage.

It outlines how contraception is in direct conflict with the Creator's plan for marriage. Such conflict brings its own unhappiness, whether the spouses hold religious beliefs or not. This book illustrates how contraception is an insidious, potent, undermining factor to marital intimacy and harmony.

Does this mean I am advocating an endless stream of children? Certainly not. Every couple has a duty to exercise 'responsible parenthood'. There are key decisions in the area of our intimate marital relations that will powerfully draw us together as spouses or drive us apart. If these decisions are made correctly, and spouses are blessed with the ability to conceive, children will arrive at a time and frequency best

> *Do you want a marriage that you know will hold together as long as you live?*

suited to each marriage and its circumstances.

Am I suggesting that every couple who uses contraception is destined to break up? No I'm not. Break-up in marriage is much more complex than that. There are many reasons for such a tragic scenario – familial, social, personal, spiritual and circumstantial.

However, I am saying that a marriage without contraception has a powerful advantage from the outset.

This book presents an introduction to some of the medical, sociological and moral dimensions of contraception. In writing it, I don't claim to be an expert in philosophy, theology or doctrine. It contains a simplified 'nuts and bolts' version of a vastly complex subject about which much more could be written.

The gift of human sexuality is a great mystery. It cannot be treated in sound bites or crude clichés.

To my Protestant brothers and sisters

What would Jesus Christ say about contraception? That is a key question for all Christians, Catholic or non-Catholic. Would He have advocated the pill to married couples struggling with finances or marital difficulties? Is contraception part of God's plan for life, marriage and family?

It is true that contemporary Evangelical Christianity, broadly speaking, regards contraception as acceptable in modern day life. However, there is a substantial basis, biblical and otherwise, for re-examining this perception.

While the Bible doesn't directly state that "contraception is right" or "contraception is wrong", it does give us clear indications that contraception is contrary to God's will. The book of Ephesians Chapter 5 outlines how Christian marriage between husband and wife in a mysterious way reflects the relationship of Christ and His bride, the Church.

He exemplified for us that love, real spousal love, means laying down one's life in total self-giving for another. Is it conceivable that Christ would contemplate a contraceptive-type mentality in His love for his bride?

Some modern day Protestants who question or oppose contraception are cited within this book. The 'Marriage' and 'Contraception' sections draw principally from scripture and Catholic Church documents. While it is true that Roman Catholics are bound to follow Church teaching in all matters in order to be Catholics of good standing, non-Catholic Christians do not regard themselves so bound.

May I suggest to my Protestant brothers and sisters in Christ and to all my readers, as you read this book, consider a different perspective. Look at the history and origin of contraception. Consider the medical and statistical evidence outlined in this book.

Examine the link between marital harmony and respect for the natural events of the female monthly cycle. Weigh the quotations and citations. How do the concepts resonate with scripture?

Consider the tree by its fruits.

Key for abbreviations

The references occurring more than once throughout this book are abbreviated at the bottom of each page along with page and/or paragraph number(s).

For example a reference from the *Catechism of the Catholic Church* paragraph 2368 is referenced by the abbreviated form (CCCn2368) at the foot of the page.

Also, the abbreviation 'cf', before a reference means refer to that reference for further information eg cfCCCn2368 means see *Cathechism of the Catholic Church* paragraph 2368 for further information. The letters 'cf' indicate in some cases that an incomplete or non exact quotation or concept is cited from the indicated source.

Here is the key for abbreviations and sources:

Allocution to Midwives	Pope Pius XII, Allocution to Italian Union of Midwives, October 29, 1951
Burke, C	Cormac Burke, *Covenanted Happiness, Love and Commitment in Marriage*, Four Courts Press, Dublin, 1990
Burke, T	Theresa Burke, *The Contraception of Grief; The Genesis of Anguish conceived by Abortifacients and Sterilisation*, Rachel's Vineyard Ministeries PA, USA www.rachelsvineyard,org
CC	*Casti Connubii*, Encyclical letter of Pope Pius XI on 'Christian Marriage' 31 Dec 1930, published by Pauline Books and Media, 50 St Paul's Avenue, Boston, MA 02130 (www.pauline.org)
CCC	*Catechism of the Catholic Church*, Geoffrey Chapman Publishers, London, A Continuum Imprint, 2000
CIC	*Code of Canon Law*, (Codex Iuris Canonici) 1983, Collins, London
de Stoop	Christine de Stoop. *Contraception – The Hidden Truth*, Castle Hill 2158, NSW, Australia
Drogin	Elasah Drogin, *Margaret Sanger, Father of Modern Society*. New Hope KY: CUL Publications, 1980
EV	*Evangelium Vitae*, Pope John Paul II, Encyclical Letter - The Gospel of Life - On the Value and Inviolability of Human Life, March 25, 1995
FC	*Familiaris Consortio*, Apostolic Exhortation of Pope John Paul II on the Role of the Christian Family in the Modern World, 22nd November 1981, published by Pauline Books and Media as above
Grant	George Grant, *Grand Illusion, The Legacy of Planned Parenthood*, 3rd Ed, Highland Books 1998. Used with

	permission.
GS	*Gaudium et Spes*, Pastoral Constitution, Second Vatican Council, 'On the Church in the Modern World', 7th December 1965.
HV	*Humanae Vitae*, Encyclical letter of Paul VI 'Of Human Life' issued July 25,1968, published by Pauline Books and Media
Kippley, Art of NFP	JohnF. & Sheila Kippley, *The Art of Natural Family Planning*, 4th ed., Couple to Couple League, USA, 1996
Kippley, BCCD	John F. Kippley, *Birth Control and Christian Discipleship*, 2nd edition, Couple to Couple League, Ohio, 1994
Kippley, SMC	John F. Kippley, *Sex and the Marriage Covenant* Couple to Couple League, Ohio, 1991
LF	*Letter to Families*, Pope John Paul II, 1994, published by Pauline Books and Media as above
LR	*Love and Responsibility*, Karol Wojtyla, First English Translation, Fount Paperbacks, Harper Collins, London 1981
Marshall & Donovan	R. Marshall & C. Donovan, *Blessed are the Barren – The Social Policy of Planned Parenthood*, Ignatius Press, San Francisco, 1991
McDonald	Deacon Dr Bob McDonald, *What Contraception does to Marriage*, conference address,Pandora's Pill Box conference 1999, The Gift Foundation, PO Box 95, Carpentersville, IL USA, www.giftfoundation.org
MD	*Mulieris Dignitatem*, Pope John Paul II's Apostolic Letter on the Dignity and Vocation of Women, issued August 15th 1988
Michael	Robert T. Michael, Why did the U.S. Divorce rate Double within a Decade? *Research in Population Economics*, vol 6, p367-399, 1988
Provan	Charles D. Provan, *The Bible and Birth Control*, Monongahela, PA. Zimmer, 1989 p81
Shivanandan	Mary Shivanandan, *Crossing the Threshold of Love – A New Vision for Marriage*, Cua Press, Washington, USA, 1999, Used with permission : The Catholic University of America Press, Washington DC
Smith	Janet E. Smith, *Why Humanae Vitae was right: A Reader*, Ignatius Press, 1993
TOB	*Theology of the Body – Human Love in the Divine Plan.* Pope John Paul II, Reprinted by The Daughters of St Paul, Pauline Books and Media as above
Torode	Samuel & Bethany Torode, *Open Embrace: A Protestant Couple Rethinks Contraception*, W.B. Eerdmans Publishing Co., 2002, available to order online at www.omsoul.com
Vademecum	*Vademecum for Confessors Concerning Some Aspects of the*

                    Morality of Conjugal Life,
                    Pontificial Council for the Family, Vatican City 12th
                    February 1997

VandeVusse   VandeVusse, L., Fehring R.J. et al, "Couples' Views
                    on the effects of Natural Family Planning on Marital
                    Dynamics", *Journal of Nursing Scholarship,* 2003; 35:2,
                    171-176;

West   Christopher West, *Good News about Sex and Marriage,*
                    Servant (Charis) Publications, Ohio, 2000

Wilson   Mercedes Wilson, *The Practice of Natural Family
                    Planning vs the Use of Artificial Birth Control: Family,
                    Sexual and Moral Issues,* Catholic Social Science
                    Review, Vol VII, Nov 2002

Part One

The Beauty of Marriage, Family and Sexuality

Chapter One

The Ideal of Marriage

Where Christ truly reigns, a marriage will bear the full characteristics of authentic love; it is 'fully human', 'free', entails 'total' self-giving, is 'faithful', utterly 'exclusive' until death and is 'fruitful'.

cf Humanae Vitae n9

My Own Story

She was walking in front of me out of a meeting in New York. This beautiful young woman, radiant, full of life, love, smiles and chat was to become – though I didn't realise it at the time - my wife within ten months. We were part of a six strong team from Ireland who had been invited to work with government delegates at the United Nations.

Suddenly, as I walked behind her, the tune of a hymn flashed across my mind. It was a tune I hadn't heard for years;

"Your wife will be like a fruitful vine within your house... your sons will be as branches around your table... so the man who fears the Lord is blest."

"This can't be true!" I thought to myself in disbelief. "She's so beautiful... Surely God isn't telling me something!!?? Surely it doesn't relate to HER!... Your wife!? – a fruitful vine!? – sons!? - my children – with her!!??"

Despite my surprise and disbelief that it could be true, at a deeper level, I admitted to myself: "WOW! Children with HER! That would be WONDERFUL!!!!!"

Prompting from God?

Was this experience in New York a prompting from God? While being slow to ascribe such an experience to God, with the benefit of hindsight, I now think it was – the most wonderful prompt of my life. And if it WAS God, even then he was speaking to me *about my future children*.

Deep down in my heart, at that moment, I knew implicitly that marriage would mean children. Deep down, subconsciously, I said 'Yes'.

I have often thought of that moment. At the time of writing, we have four children here and four others who have gone to God through miscarriage. I tell this story because I believe it points to an extremely important truth. That truth is that God is looking for married couples who are willing to say 'yes' to children, 'yes' to love, 'yes' to life.

God, I believe, is excited about marriage and desires to bless you and your chosen spouse. He is longing for you to know real love and harmony with your spouse.

I don't often experience God speaking to me directly but I have had a few other similar experiences which I will relate in later pages. Interestingly, some of them related to my future wife and children as well.

The Wedding

Do you remember the joy and thrill of getting married? That feeling of longing, of waiting to have your beloved as your very own, of wanting to be one with them in everything? I do. Do you remember waking up on your wedding morning? (The morning that you often wondered as a single person would it ever happen to you?). The day you said 'Yes' to the love of your dreams and your beloved saying 'I do' to you at the altar? I do! How could you ever forget?

Do you remember the anticipation and excitement, the prospects and goals, the desire to be together and share the joys and burdens of life? Do you remember the longing to share the same house, the same table and the same bed as your beloved?

The day arrives... the ceremony... the reception... the speeches... the evening celebrations... and thus began the most intimate relationship of my life with all its challenges, joys and enrichment!

The start of a new life you've always longed for! Where is it going? Who will be there? How will we fare?

The Ideal of Marriage

I believe that the ideal of marriage, that is of permanent unity, complete fidelity, life-long friendship, love, tenderness and harmony, is realistic and possible in your marriage. You can still feel crazy about your spouse and see that 'sparkle' in your beloved's eyes for YOU in thirty or more years time.

WHY? Because with God, *"all things are possible"*.[1] Through the sacramental graces of your marriage, Christ the author of marriage has pledged an unending flow of sanctifying grace to help you, no matter how difficult the circumstances that life may throw at you.

I believe that God wants your marriage

> God, I believe, is looking for married couples that are willing to say 'Yes' to children, 'Yes' to love, 'Yes' to life

---

[1] Lk 1:37

to succeed, to last the course and to be a source of joy and harmony to yourselves and everyone else whose lives you touch. I believe He has pledged His power and His presence to walk with you every step of the way – counselling, instructing, guiding, comforting and easing the way. He calls us, and helps us, to strive towards perfection in our marriages. All of us in our marriages are on a journey towards perfection.

The Maker's Instructions

Everyone desires happiness but where does it come from? The scriptures and the Church, with 2000 years of experience on earth, tell us that true happiness comes from obedience to God's laws. The Church notes:

> "Man cannot attain that true happiness for which he yearns with all the strength of his spirit, unless he keeps the laws which the Most High God has engraved in his very nature. These laws must be wisely and lovingly observed." [1]

If you buy a car and carefully follow the maker's instructions, you can be assured you will get a satisfactory performance, a long life and a good return. However, if you don't follow the maker's instructions and try to do things your own way – like using diesel in an engine where the manufacturer specifies petrol, the car won't go very far. The manufacturer has put a lot of thought into producing his car. He knows how it works. His instructions help you get the best performance from your purchase.

Marriage is similar. God made marriage and when we follow the Maker's instructions, it is our best chance for happiness. We get the best possible return. Christ tells us "Happy are those who hear the word of God and obey it!" [2]

He has bestowed upon marriage a structure, a pattern, and sound principles, which if followed faithfully -with HIS grace - will help you enormously in attaining the ideals.

Obedience to God's laws, including His plan for the number of children He wishes to bless us with, is the best chance we give ourselves to achieve marital fulfillment and peace.

> "Man cannot attain ... true happiness ... unless he keeps the laws which... God has engraved in his very nature."
> cf HVn31

---

[1] HVn31
[2] Lk 11:28

A Survey

What group of women do you think had the following results in a poll?

✓ a dramatically low divorce rate
✓ experienced happier marriages
✓ were happier and more satisfied in their everyday lives
✓ had considerably more marital intercourse
✓ shared a deeper intimacy with their spouse
✓ realised a deeper level of communication
✓ incorporated prayer more in their daily lives
✓ relied strongly on the teachings of the Church, the Bible and Almighty God
✓ were personally happier
✓ had strong traditional, social and moral views
✓ preserved the family unit better than the other groups
✓ were unlikely to have had an abortion
✓ were unlikely to have cohabitated
✓ were less likely to work full-time
✓ were unlikely to be supportive of or engage in sexual intercourse outside of marriage

Who were these women? They were a group of women who did not use contraception in their marriages but practiced natural family planning instead.[1] (Natural family planning is not to be confused with the out-of-date, unreliable 'rhythm method').

This list is an indicator of a key stabilising factor in marriage – avoidance of contraception. There is a more thorough discussion of the use of natural methods of family planning later in this book.

Where Christ Truly Reigns

A marriage where Christ truly reigns will bear the hallmarks of His presence: love, joy, peace, patience, kindness, generosity, faithfulness, gentleness and self-control.[2] Where He truly reigns, a marriage will bear the characteristics of authentic love; it is 'fully human', 'free', entails 'total' self-giving, is 'faithful', utterly 'exclusive' until death and is 'fruitful'.[3] That is the ideal. All of us fall short, sometimes very short.

But the call to strive for perfection and to better ourselves is open to us all and the means to achieve this are accessible. The grace of our marriage sacrament is ever present.

True happiness, the *Catechism of the Catholic Church* adds, is found:

---

[1] Wilson, Mercedes Arzu., The Culture of Life: Presuppositions and Dimensions, General Assembly of the Pontifical Acadamy for Life, March 2001, quoted in *The Contraception of Grief* by Theresa Burke, Rachel's Vineyard Ministries, PA, USA www.rachelsvineyard.org
[2] cf Gal 5: 22-23
[3] cf HV n9

"in God alone, the source of every good and of all love." [1]

It is Christ who is:

"... the source of unity and peace." [2]

Wouldn't you want the source of 'unity and peace', the source of 'every good and all love', Christ himself, at the heart of YOUR marriage?

The Best for YOUR Marriage

The modern world has cultivated a negativity about children. The expense! The strain! The loss of independence! The sleeplessness! The crying! The mortgage payments! Overpopulation! All my education will be wasted! Will I cope?

As a result many couples enter marriages reluctant to have children too soon, too often or any at all. Children are not seen as a priceless gift but as a wearisome burden. With the worry of having an unwanted child, many couples resort to contraception to avoid having children.

This is a sad mistake because, as revealed later in this book, the presence of small children actually enhances a married couple's chances of staying together, especially when the marriage is tested. Children have a most definite part in enhancing marriage.

I believe that God wants exactly what is best for you and your spouse. He has THE perfect family size for YOU. Every couple is different and every family is different.

God's plan for your family size will be exactly right for your circumstances, abilities and personalities. He already knows what the personality of each of your children will be. To some families He will send just one child; to others more, to some, perhaps none will arrive.

He knows what combination of children to send that will best ensure your chances of reaching your ultimate heavenly destiny. Our job is to be sure we are closely following His plan. It may mean re-evaluating some of our priorities.

'Perfect love casts out fear' [3] the scriptures remind us. Fear of children has no part in a Catholic or Christian marriage. God wants us to enjoy a life of marital intimacy free from crippling fears of unwanted children. He promises to set us free from such fear.

How Much is REALLY Understood?

So how much do newly-weds really understand when they say 'yes' at the altar? If you were like me, you were more interested on your wedding day in getting on with loving your beloved than having to work through the legalities, the formalities, the ecclesial language, the technical requirements of Church and State.

---

[1] CCCn1723

[2] Pope Paul VI *Lumen Gentium*, Dogmatic Constitution on the Church, n9, Nov 21 1964

[3] 1Jn 4:18

Yes, I believed marriage was forever. There was no second chance. There was no going back. (Growing up, my dad told us repeatedly as children that when you got married you get "*only one bite of the cherry*").

I knew my wife and I had to accept any children God might send us and that the Catholic Church taught contraception was wrong. I'd read that natural family planning had been scientifically proven as reliable. It was also morally acceptable. I also believed we needed Christ at the centre of our marriage...

But I didn't *fully* understand WHY contraception was wrong, why every act of marital intercourse had to be open to conception. I wasn't exactly sure why marriage was indissoluble, why the words of consent at the altar were so profoundly important in God's eyes. I didn't fully realise why the total self-giving of marital intercourse was so heavily laden with symbolism, though I did understand that having children was a core mission of every married couple.

Since then I have discovered that these things are essential and fundamental for a faithful, fruitful, joy-filled marriage that will endure. I started to read and talk with other married couples. Only then did I discover how destructive contraception can be to marital harmony.

I started to read and talk with other married couples. Only then did I discover how destructive contraception can be to marital harmony.

Chapter Two

What is Marriage All About?

An elderly couple celebrating their 50th anniversary of marriage were asked how they managed to stay together for fifty years. They replied "We got married!'"

Everyone is Created to Love

A young couple in love, all dressed up for an evening out, are walking along a pier in the evening sunshine after a meal in a restaurant. He turns to her and says: "If I jump into the sea, would you jump in after me?" She thinks he's not being serious and says "of course I would".

So he jumps, clothes and all, into the sea. She looks at him in horror. Then a smile appears across her face. She slowly bends to remove her shoes and jumps in after him in her evening dress.

That is romance! That is excitement and adventure! It's literally taking the plunge! This is the thrill every couple wants to feel throughout their married life.

Take a walk in your local park on a sunny evening and look at the young couples in love and feel their energy and excitement. See the middle aged couples alone and those with children and feel their love. There's an elderly couple, occasionally glancing into each other's eyes with that look of love.

Love, love, love! It's what we were created for. Pope John Paul II said that love is the fundamental, innate vocation of every person, each of whom is made in the image of God.[1]

There's no getting away from it. We are made for love, with God and each other. It is the same for every person - married or single.

However, the essence of love and marriage isn't about the thrill, the romance or the feelings.

What is Marriage?

The following definition by author and speaker Christopher West, derived from Catholic Church documents, is hard to better:

---

[1] cf FCn11

29

> *"Marriage is the intimate, exclusive, indissoluble communion of life and love entered by man and woman at the design of the Creator for the purpose of their own good and the procreation and education of children; this covenant between baptized persons has been raised by Christ the Lord to the dignity of a sacrament."* [1]

Each word and phrase of this definition is loaded with significance and meaning. It is crucial that every engaged and married couple understand what they are saying "I do" to when they give their consent at the altar.

What 'Makes' a Marriage?

So what is it that man and woman say 'I do' to? What are they signing up for? Precisely what makes them husband and wife? What 'happens' at that moment? As well as the words of consent pledged at the altar, the Catholic Church identifies three essential components of marriage.[2] They are:

1) UNITY - exclusive faithfulness

2) CHILDREN - openness to fertility and

3) INDISSOLUBILITY - marriage is for life

Marriage is about lifelong unity and procreation.[3] You get married in order to be one with your spouse, to have children and to raise a family. Each spouse marries for the lifelong good of the other, to lay down their life for the other, for mutual enrichment and the enrichment of their children if they are so blessed. That's what marriage is about.

Personal Experience

I have to confess that when I was praying for a wife, I was seeking a woman who wanted to be a full-time wife and mother. I was blessed to marry a woman who shared such a vision and who was also competent in so many other areas as well.

She had many skills and abilities - organising youth retreats in schools and retreat centres, working as a special needs teaching assistant, accreditation in counselling and educated to technical college level. She was experienced in public speaking, in desktop publishing, computing and guitar playing. She has travelled widely. She brought all these talents and more to the service of her marriage and family.

She understood that marriage was about laying down your life for the good of your spouse and children. Marriage to her was to be her primary vocation - it did not mean a job in the workplace first and fitting in a family second. The same

---

[1] West, p46 ; cf GSn48; cf CCC1603; cf CICn1055
[2] cf CCCn1643-4
[3] cf HVn12

30

goes for husbands. I have come to see that when we men get married, our wives and children – our vocation – are more important, than our jobs.

The Symbolism of Married Love

Did you know that the love of husband and wife reflects the relationship between Christ and His Church? Marriage between two baptized persons *"is a real symbol of the union of Christ and the Church."*[1] That makes marriage indissoluble just as Christ's commitment to HIS bride, the Church, is *"eternally faithful."* [2]

Not only that, did you know that the love and communion of husband and wife is designed by the Creator to reflect on earth the generous, life-giving, loving nature of God in the Blessed Trinity? [3,4]

St. Paul highlights how Christ's love for the Church is the model for marital love:

> *"Husbands should love their wives just as Christ loved the Church and sacrificed himself for her to make her holy."* [5]

Marital love is thus FREE, TOTAL, FAITHFUL, EXCLUSIVE and FRUITFUL.[6] Christ showed these five characteristics of love to perfection during His life on earth. This is the type of love every couple is called to in their marriage.

---

[1] FCn80

[2] cf FCn80; cf FCn20

[3] cf CCCn2335; cf MDn7; cf TOBp469; cf LFn6-8

[4] The mystery of the Most Holy Trinity is the central mystery of the Christian faith in which three persons: Father, Son and Holy Spirit exist as one God in the mystery of a perfect communion of love (cfCCCn253 - 256)

[5] Eph5:25; cfCCCn1659

[6] cfHVn9

Just what are we saying "*I do*" to
when we get married ?

"*I do*" want a fab wedding with all
my pals... "*I do*" want a huge house...
"*I do*" want lots of 'me' time... "*I do*"
want at least 3 sun holidays a year...
"*I do*" want my own bank account...
"*I do*" want to keep my career
centre-stage...

BRIDE No. 1

BRIDE No. 2

The Church on Sexuality

The gift of sexuality is a wonderful thing. It is no accident that the Creator crafted man and woman to be so anatomically different and yet so gloriously complementary in even the physical aspect of their bodies.

When expressed in its fullest and proper manner, the act of marital intercourse between husband and wife (henceforth referred to in this book as the 'marital act') is deeply symbolic and is an enthralling and deeply joyous encounter. It is one of the delights of marriage intended by God to be exclusively enjoyed by spouses.[1]

The Catholic Church has a thoroughly positive view of sexual intercourse exercised in its proper place:

> "The acts in marriage, by which the intimate and chaste union of spouses takes place are noble and honourable. The truly human performance of these acts fosters the self-giving they signify and enriches the spouses in joy and gratitude. Sexuality is a source of joy and pleasure." [2]

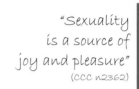

"Sexuality is a source of joy and pleasure" (CCC n2362)

Symbolism of the Marital Act
"I give my all to you"

The marital act bodily symbolises the union and the total self-giving that marriage represents. Indeed, the total self-giving of husband and wife to each other in the act symbolises the total self-giving of Christ to HIS bride, the Church. Between spouses, it is the fleshly embodiment of those words of consent at the altar: *"I take you as my wife"* ; *"I take you as my husband."* In this act of mutual love, each spouse uniquely gives of themselves to the other in a profound way as 'gift' – the total gift of self. Each receives the other as a gift.[3] Each act is, in effect, a renewal of their marriage covenant.[4]

Total Self-giving Means New Life

It is no secret that the marital act is orientated **to having** babies. By logic, it is not hard to see how the total self-giving of the marital act between husband and wife implicitly involves, even on a physical level, an openness to procreation.[5]

In every marital act, each of the spouses 'says' with their body:

---

[1] cf CCCn2390; cf CCn18; cf "Allocution to Midwives" 1951, cf HVn8
[2] CCCn2362
[3] cf TOBp69-72; LFn12; cf GSn49; cf FCn32
[4] cf Kippley SMC p7
[5] cf LFn12

"I surrender my whole self to you – body and personage, wholly and totally - that I give the very seed within me, to be united with yours. I give myself so much to you – to receive all of you - that I am willing to co-parent with you a new 'us', a new being, the fruit of our mutual love - a child." [1]

Why is Marriage to be Fruitful?

I was videoed the night before my wedding. At one point I say directly to the camera 'Hi Children' to my future children. I wasn't being presumptuous; it was an expression of my excitement and openness to having them. I was madly in love with my beautiful wife-to-be and why wouldn't I want to have lots of children with her?

There are a number of reasons that provide a coherent basis for understanding why marriage is implicitly orientated to fruitfulness by procreation.

Firstly, when God spoke to Adam and Eve, the very first husband and wife, He blessed them and gave the command:

> *"Be fruitful and multiply, and fill*
> *the earth and subdue it."* [2]

This command and invitation of God – the Creator and Institutor of marriage Himself - to mankind to *'be fruitful and multiply'* is a key component to marriage since its origin and is extended to every married couple today. [3]

Secondly, the total self-giving in the marital act inherently involves an openness to procreation. Married love, reflecting Christ's relationship with His bride the Church, is intended by God to be implicitly fruitful because Christ's love for the Church is supremely fruitful. [4]

Thirdly, spouses in their communion and procreation of their children reflect the generous, life-giving Trinitarian nature of God towards all His creation. [5] Marriage by its very nature and structure is orientated to procreation.

> *This command by God to mankind - to 'go forth and multiply' is an implicit part of marriage.*

---

[1] cf Cormac Burke, *Marriage and Contraception*; cf Smith, J., *Why Humanae Vitae was Right*. Ignatius Press 1993 p157

[2] LFn6;cf TOBp50; Genesis 1:28;CCn11;CCn34

[3] cf CCn11;CCn34

[4] cf HVn8,n9; cf CCCn808

[5] cf TOBp469; cf CCCn2367

The Blessed Trinity in Heaven is reflected by husband, wife and children on earth

Thus, to have children (procreation) and to ensure their formation and education is the 'proper mission', 'most serious duty', an 'honor' or 'primary obligation'[1] of married couples.[2]

Openness to children is a principal component of marriage. In consenting with the words "I do" each spouse is implicitly accepting and receiving the 'whole' of the other person, fertility included, and all the consequences that may flow from that.[3]

Marriage Can Be a Challenge

I remember my wife Therese and I had some serious and painful arguments, particularly in our second year of marriage.

The flush of romantic enchantment was wearing off, the second child had arrived, sleep was in short supply and reality had begun to bite. Two strong, independent wills clashed repeatedly. Neither of us had ever been forced to face up to the 'self' lurking within in such a way before.

Never before had we been in such close proximity to another person to such a degree – and to someone we'd pledged to love and make sacrifice for until the end of our lives! This was 'carrying the cross' like we'd never experienced before.

---

[1] NB The 'primary obligation' to have children does not mean an absolute obligation to have children in every circumstance as explained in Chapter Fourteen 'Seven Key Principles of Responsible Parenthood'

[2] cf CCCn2367; cf CCCn1652-1653;cf HVn1; GSn50, *Vademecum for confessors* n2:2; Allocution to Midwives 1951;cf Smith, A Reader p454; cf HVn10

[3] cf HVn10

Marriage Helps Root Out Selfishness

Marriage, the Church teaches, is *"a grace"* given to us by God to help us overcome the selfishness within every one of us.[1]

> *"...marriage helps to overcome self-absorption, egoism, pursuit of one's own pleasure and to open oneself to the other, to mutual aid and to self-giving."* [2]

Let's be clear, the ultimate goal of this life on earth is eternal life in heaven with God.[3] In marriage, a sacrament is established which empowers spouses with the grace for the duties of married life.[4] It strengthens their unity, perfects their love and sanctifies them on the way to eternal life.[5]

At the time of those earlier painful struggles in our marriage, we were assured by those more experienced that every couple reaches this juncture in their marriage to some degree. It is an important growth phase in the life of each marriage. Establishment of clear, recognised principles of good communication at this point is key. How well or how badly a married couple make their choices in such a growth phase has an extremely important bearing on their future harmony and peace with one another.

The Dignity of Children in Marriage

As parents, husband and wife are elevated to the role of co-workers with the Author of Life Himself.

When God sends the gift of a child, parents receive a priceless charge, whose inexpressible dignity is linked to his sacred origin and final eternal destiny with God.[6] Mum and dad are entrusted with the stewardship of an unspeakable treasure of whose care they will one day have to give account.[7]

Children are not something to be feared in marriage. They are the *"crowning glory"* of marriage and *"contribute greatly to the good of the parents themselves."* [8] The benefit of children to marriage we will examine in the next section.

It is important that parents seek to be in harmony with the will of God in having each new child.[9] Children are not a right, they are a gift from God. Parents are co-creators, not the creators.

What a fantastic privilege and responsibility!! What a high office marriage is. Marriage should not to be undertaken lightly. God holds marriage in very high esteem!

---

[1] cf TOBp347-348
[2] CCCn1609
[3] cf CCCn1024
[4] cf CCCn1661;cf CCCn774
[5] cf CCCn1661
[6] cf EVn38;cfLFn9
[7] cf CCn15
[8] cf CCCn1652;GSn48-50
[9] cf LFn9

Children are not something to be feared in marriage. They are its "crowning glory".

37

Chapter Three

How Children Strengthen Marriage

"When I was getting married I didn't take children seriously. They weren't a feature in my mind."

Elaine, mother

My Future Descendents

Years before I even knew my future wife, I believe God was speaking to me about my future children.

At that difficult time as a pharmacist in making the decision to stop dispensing the contraceptive pill in 1993, I was praying one day when I was struck by a verse of scripture that changed my life forever:

> *"See, I set before you life or death, blessing or curse; choose life that you and your descendents might live."* [1]

Through this verse of scripture, I felt God was giving me a choice. The choice was to stop dispensing the pill which would lead me to 'life' and 'blessing', or to continue dispensing it, which somehow would have me interface with 'death' and 'curse'. I felt God was exhorting me to 'choose life' and that somehow my decision would mean life for me and my future descendents.

I made the decision to stop dispensing the pill and other contraceptives, a decision which resulted in three years of unemployment. No-one wanted to employ a pharmacist who wouldn't dispense the pill. Having written my first book on contraception at that time, I was offered employment in the pro-life movement in the Republic of Ireland in 1997, the year I met the girl who would become my future wife. I was invited to speak as a pharmacist on the subject of the abortifacient nature of the contraceptive pill at a youth retreat in Dublin, a retreat which she organised.

Three years later we started dating and now eight children who are enormous blessings have been bestowed upon us - the *crowning glory of marriage* the Church calls them.

I may never have had those eight children if I had ignored what God was calling me to do all those years ago regarding dispensing the pill. He knows the future; He knows what is best.

---

[1] Deuteronomy 30:19

Children Are a Blessing

Scripture tell us that children are like arrows in the hand of a warrior.[1] They are a 'reward' from God. *"Blessed is the man whose quiver is full of them."* [2]

To the man who fears God the scriptures say:

> *"Your wife will be like a fruitful vine within your house; your sons will be like olive shoots around your table."* [3]

There's that word 'fruitful' again. The Papal encyclical *Casti Connubii* proclaims: *"Among the blessings of marriage, the child holds the first place."* [4] The *Catechism* tells us that children are the supreme gift of marriage and benefit parents greatly." [5]

_____

[1] cf Ps127:3-5
[2] cf Ps127:5
[3] Ps128:3-4 NIV
[4] CCn11
[5] cf CCCn1652;GSn50

Children Strengthen Marriage

Now let's explore some evidence on the beneficial effects of children on a marriage.

"Shared sacrifice is one of the best bonds of love"

writes Monsignor Cormac Burke in his thought-provoking book *Covenanted Happiness, Love and Commitment in Marriage.* He notes:

> *"Children can and do draw from parents a degree of sacrifice to which neither parent, alone, could probably inspire the other... In this way, as they sacrifice themselves for their children, each parent actually improves and becomes – in their partner's eyes also – truly a more lovable person."* [1]

My wife tells me that the arrival of our children brought out some things in me she hadn't seen before. In her eyes, I was 'Mr Sensible', especially in our earlier years. She was pleasantly surprised to discover that when the children began to arrive I was actively involved with them. Rough and tumble play is an important role for me to fulfil! In her own words, my involvement in the children's upbringing strengthened her love and regard for me. She said the children made me more loving (and even more lovable!).

Children Result in Less Marriage Break-up

In the statistical research of economist and social scientist Robert T. Michael, the presence of a young child in the house meant a 30% lower divorce rate for couples married between 5-15 years.[2] The addition of a second child lowered the likelihood of divorce a further 30%.

In his professional and practical experience in dealing with applications for annulments from Catholic married couples, Rev. Burke makes a striking observation:

> *"In my work at the Roman Rota, I not infrequently come across petitions of annulment of what clearly are perfectly genuine marriages of couples who married out of love, but whose marriages collapsed fundamentally because they deliberately delayed having children and thus deprived their mutual love of its natural support."* [3]

In Rev. Burke's experience the deliberate delaying of having children can cause marriages to collapse. Conversely, the stability of marriages increases with the presence of children. Why is this so? Do children solidify the attachment and union that comes from the conjugal act?

A child requires commitment from mum and dad to accept together the joys, demands and strains that such a new life entails. In the author's own

---

[1] Burke, C p24
[2] cf Michael p377
[3] Burke, C p46

41

experience the desire to ensure the happiness of one's children is a pointed stimulus for mum and dad to stick it through the difficulties, and actively pursue the strengthening of marital harmony. Children are like glue for a marriage.

Higher Levels of Self-giving

Here's a young mother's thoughts on the role children play in drawing mum and dad to higher levels of tolerance and self-giving:

> *"We have five young children – we are so close together – the whole point of life is the family. As parents, you learn tolerance, care and the sense of security. You discover just who you are. Yes, it's true. Children bring you to the limit of your patience and back; often it's uncivilised, the tiredness, no sleep, no time for yourself.*
>
> *It strips away all the social fluff that you go into marriage with. You learn how to really cherish the other; you see just how REALLY committed to the other you are. Your mettle is being tested in the fire. You discover what you're REALLY like – what your spouse is like.*
>
> *You get exhausted past the point of being reasonable but you just get up again. That's just the way it is – you happily put yourself last. I'll suffer if I have to, but this is what it's all about. It's unrelenting; you couldn't be paid to do it. But mothers are just getting quietly on with it everywhere.*
>
> *However, the whole concept of family is so perfect that it can only be divine – on every level – social, educational, spiritual, every angle and facet. The sacrifice strengthens who you are, who you both are!* [1]

Children are unifying when romance begins to fade. Rev. Burke further makes the observation that:

> *"It seems to me that one of the most obvious, frequent and saddest mistakes of many young couples today embarking on marriage is the decision to postpone having any children for a number of years – two or three or five – after getting married. The result is that precisely in that moment when romance starts to fade, when their love begins to run into difficulties and needs support, the main support which nature thought of (had "planned" I would say) for that moment – their children – does not exist".* [2]

Parenting... "strips away all the social fluff that you go into marriage with..."

The absence of children can cause couples to become discontented with each other. Rev. Burke states:

---

[1] EM Personal communication Feb 2007
[2] Burke, Cp25

"If two people remain just looking ecstatically into each other's eyes, the defects that little by little they are going to discover there can eventually begin to appear intolerable. If they gradually learn to look out together at their children, they will still discover each other's defects, but they have less time or reason to think them intolerable. They cannot however look out together at what is not there." [1]

The Dignity of Motherhood

Here is the story of a young woman who underwent a transformation on the importance of her motherhood with the arrival of her first child:

"When I was getting married I didn't take children seriously. They weren't a feature in my mind. My husband-to-be came from a big family and wanted children and I agreed with that in our discussions. However, I didn't take on board the seriousness of that commitment.

A few months after we got married, I realised I was pregnant. I cried and cried. My husband thought there was a death in the family. I felt trapped. Up to the birth of our first child I felt really angry. "I didn't plan for you" was my attitude. I idolised my husband Emmet. "Who do you think you are coming between Emmet and I?" To me the baby was like a cuckoo in the nest. I didn't know if I wanted him or not.

However, as the pregnancy progressed, I found myself wanting to know more. I got a book on pregnancy – I had a hunger for knowledge – I wanted to know the technicalities of life in the womb. I was amazed by what I read.

Before the birth, I went out of my way to secure my maternity rights and planned to return to work a few weeks after the birth. I phoned crèches and had everything ready.

When Paul arrived, everything changed. I just looked at him and realised "That's MY little person. I'm the only person who can love him like I can". I couldn't stand the idea of a crèche.

Everything about work became totally irrelevant. At 25, I was the third youngest female accountant for a prestigious hotel chain. I was away ahead of most men in my field. When I became a mother, I couldn't have cared less about anyone's stupid accounts. "This is my child – this is what life's all about!"

I didn't feel like a 'stupid housewife'. I felt really proud. I could see how I and almost everybody else had got it wrong. How could I have possibly

> *"I was the third youngest female accountant for a prestigious hotel chain at age 25... When I became a mother, I couldn't care less about anyone's stupid accounts"*

---

[1] Burke C p46

bonded with him if I only had him for an hour in the morning before leaving him in a crèche?" [1]

This young mother underwent a transformation regarding the dignity of motherhood when her first child arrived. The role of motherhood – and especially full-time motherhood - has been hugely undermined by the world around us.

It is true that many mothers are compelled to work through sheer force of circumstances. It is true that many women have talents that can benefit the community and to use these talents outside the home is truly meritorious. Women in all walks of life contribute immeasurably to the enrichment of society. However, when children arrive, many mothers realise how their priorities have changed.

Motherhood is one of the highest callings in life. Each man has a key role to play in upholding his wife's role as mother and primary caregiver to his children.

Child-rearing Can Indeed be Tough

While every child is a blessing, that's not to say child-rearing isn't difficult. Let's be realistic - crying babies, parental exhaustion, sleepless nights, the demands of breast or bottle feeding, nappy-changing, demands for attention, interruption of adult conversation, discipline issues, education, child character formation, the loss of freedom of our single, carefree days - all these are a real test of our individual resolve and marital commitment.

The tension within ourselves between selfishness and other-centredness is sorely tested in each one of us as parents. There is real suffering involved and a danger, if we are not careful, that the selfishness that lurks within each of us may overcome the sacrificial love that marriage demands.[2] Just coping can be difficult.

That's why parents are exhorted to continually turn their hearts and thoughts to God, to draw the power to continually renew their love.[3]

After Two or Three 'it gets easier'

Several parents of large families told us the most difficult time was when they had 2-3 children. After that, it got easier. Mum and dad become more adept. Siblings start to play with each other. The older children start to help. Household rhythms for child-rearing have been established and it is easier to respond to the needs of another baby.

It is around that figure of two or three children however when many couples decide they cannot cope with any more and they consciously stop having children.

I recently heard of a lady who gave birth to her fourth child, and received more expressions of sympathy for her 'plight' than she did congratulations. She had been delighted with the new arrival, but soon discovered that many people

---

[1] Emmet and Elaine, Personal communication, February 2007
[2] cf LFn7
[3] cf LFn7

44

around her viewed children as a burden. This attitude shows a sad loss of sense of value of a child! The Christian community surely has a role in supporting and encouraging mothers in their vocation.

A mother of five told us recently that if you feel you cannot cope with the demands of child-rearing, you are in a good place. It means you are forced to give up trying to do it in your OWN strength, and look to Christ for HIS strength. After all, He's the one who sent the children in the first place. He knows what's involved.

Properly understood, every suffering is a blessing and, if united to the Cross of Christ, it is redemptive. Properly received and understood, children consolidate the marital covenant between husband and wife.

Don't Be Sold Short of Even One Treasure!

God knows the perfect family size for your marriage. He is the Author of Life. Our job is to make sure we are faithful to His plan.

When God sends us a child in our marriage, he is bestowing us with treasures from his storehouse. Parents, do not allow yourselves to be sold short of even one treasure!

Consider the whoops of delight of children at Christmas. Or would any child on his birthday say to his father: "No more gifts for me dad! Two is enough!"?

Somehow, being fruitful in marriage brings our good. God didn't say: 'Go forth and replace yourselves with 2.1 children'. He said '*Go forth and MULTIPLY and fill the earth...*'.[1] It's a commandment, a directive, with a blessing attached.

The marital act is mysterious and profoundly sacred. It is so profound that spouses in this life must act with an eye to the next.[2] Every single marital act has such enormous implications for the spouses, for society and for the Kingdom of God that spouses cannot afford to get it deliberately wrong. Small wonder that Pope John Paul II speaks of spouses approaching procreation "*on one's knees.*"[3]

What a tragedy for a husband and wife to use a contraceptive one night if they unwittingly thwart the creation of a new soul destined by God as a gift to them for this life and the next.

And yet, if you ever were in this situation, God's merciful love is always available and we can contritely turn back to Him.

> "*if you feel you cannot cope with the demands of child-rearing, you are in a good place. It means that you are forced to give up trying to do it in your OWN strength, and look to Christ for HIS strength.*"
>
> *A mother*

---

[1] Genesis 1:28
[2] cf CCC n 2371
[3] LF n 7

Part Two

Contraception

Chapter Four

The History of Contraception

"Birth control appeals to the advanced radical because it is calculated to undermine the authority of the Christian Churches. I look forward to seeing humanity free someday of the tyranny of Christianity..." -

Margaret Sanger

What does the Pill Promise?

× *Freedom from Pregnancy!*

× *Spontaneity in your love life!*

× *Lots of pleasure and no responsibility*

× *Have time to enjoy life!*

× *Take Control. YOU decide when to have a baby or not!*

× *Freedom from the expense of children!*

× *Its Free! (In UK on prescription)*

How Good is Contraception?

So, the wonder drug, the glorious pill... is it really as good as all that? Apart from the side effects listed on the packet leaflet, there are other effects that are never mentioned. Some honest couples have told me that the pill is not all that it's cracked up to be. These are real life experiences, from both men and women, about using contraception. They said:

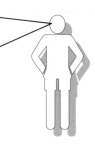

"Our sexual relationship changed from an act of marital union to a lust-filled activity... I no longer saw my wife as a person- I lost respect for her... Mary was left not feeling good... I wanted a good sex life and no hassle..."

Tom

"Things had definitely changed... there was a widening rift – a breakdown in communication... we were developing different interests... the intimate part of our marriage seemed to be dying... we didn't feel important to one another any more..."

Marie

"During this time I felt really low, really cheap. There was no communication, no hugging. It was all about physical gratification. It wasn't love. It was horrible. My self-confidence plummeted…"
Maru

"I'd grown bored with all this intercourse. Its availability every night meant it lost its specialness… there was a serious temptation to think about other women during our intimate moments…a sense of looking for fulfilment elsewhere…"
Gerard

Given the real life experience of the four people cited above, is the pill such a good thing as is commonly believed? Is there another side to the story?

Firstly, let's take a look at the history of contraception and where the contraceptive culture came from.

Early History

Examining the history and promoters of contraception reveals a lot about the ethos and ideology behind it.

Manuscripts from as far back as 2700BC in Egypt and Greece reveal contraception usage.[1] The book of Genesis records the story of a man Onan, who was slain by God for a practice we call today 'coitus interruptus' or 'withdrawal'.[2]

St. Jerome, St. John Chrysostom and St. Augustine denounced contraception in the 4th century.[3] From the 15th to the 18th centuries prominent Protestant figures such as Martin Luther, Charles Wesley and John Calvin all condemned contraceptive practices.

Modern Day Stirrings for Birth Control

Modern day stirrings in favour of birth control began with the writings of a nineteenth-century cleric named Thomas Malthus.

In his hugely influential work *"An essay on the principle of Population"*, published in six editions from 1798 to 1826, Malthus wrote that a population explosion was looming in the world, threatening imminent worldwide starvation and economic instability. The only solution, Malthus wrote, was urgent population control by whatever means necessary.

Malthus and his disciples believed that :

> *"if Western civilization were to survive, the physically unfit, the materially poor, the spiritually diseased, the racially inferior and the mentally incompetent had to somehow be suppressed and isolated – even eliminated."* [4]

Malthus went so far as to recommend the use of plague, pestilence and disease to rid the world of the so-called "unwelcome masses". He condemned charity, international relief, development, missionary outreaches and economic investment, regarding them as perpetuating the problem.

Eugenics

Some of Malthus's disciples felt a subtler approach of education, sterilisation, contraception and abortion was a better, more scientific way of addressing the situation. Malthusian thought thus laid the basis for a new 'science' called eugenics - the selective 'breeding' of the 'superior' white race, while suppressing the 'inferior' races

> *Malthus condemned charity, international relief, development, missionary outreaches and economic investment*

---

[1] cf Kippley, BCCD p2; Saunders, Fr., *The History of Contraception Teachings*, www.ewtn.com/library/answers/histcont.htm

[2] Gen 38:6-26

[3] cf www.hli.org/seminarians_eastern_orthodoxy_contraception.html

[4] as described by Grant p34

through segregation, birth control and abortion. The 'unfit' would slowly be erased and the human race would gradually become genetically 'improved'.[1]

For the next hundred years Malthus's writings became the basis for national and international social policy and research throughout the western world.

Scientists, intellectuals and social reformers were convinced of an imminent, global economic crisis caused by unchecked human fertility and the need to drastically address it.

Enter Margaret Sanger

Into this climate stepped Margaret Sanger (1879-1966) the most revolutionary person to light the birth control torch that raged around the globe in the 20th century and right up to this present day.

Born of a Catholic mother and a socialist father, by her late teens Margaret Sanger had entered into a life of radical politics, suffragette feminism, many sexual liaisons and a hatred of the Catholic Church.[2]

She openly espoused Malthusian and eugenic aims, and later became heavily involved in the occult.[3] She opened her first birth control clinic against the law of the time in Brooklyn, New York in 1916. Seeking to target the "*dysgenic immigrant Southern Europeans, Slavs, Latins and Jews*" with her birth control movement, she later sought to target "ill favoured" and "dysgenic races" such as "*Blacks, Hispanics, Amerinds, Fundamentalists, and Catholics*".[4] "*More children from the fit, less from the unfit – that is the chief aim of birth control*" was her catch-cry.[5]

In 1922 she published her best seller *The Pivot of Civilization* in which she openly called for the elimination of "*human weeds*", the segregation of "*morons, misfits and the maladjusted*", the "*cessation of charity*" and the sterilization of "*genetically inferior races.*"[6]

Radical Views

Quoting her directly best illustrates her views.
She wrote:

> "*The mass of Negroes, particularly in the South, still breed carelessly and disastrously, with the result that the increase among Negroes, even more than among whites, is from that portion of the population least intelligent and fit.*"[7]

---

[1] cf Grant p32-37

[2] Grant p65-66

[3] cf Marshall and Donovan p131

[4] Grant p40

[5] Grant p38

[6] cf Grant p37

[7] cf Grant p40

On another occasion she wrote:

> *"We do not want the word to go out that we want to exterminate the Negro population and the Minister* [of religion] *is the man who can straighten out that idea if it ever occurs to any of their more rebellious members."* [1]

Sanger's magazine *The Birth Control Review'* carried articles espousing eugenic and racist values. The headline of her December 1921 edition carried the masthead: *"Birth Control: To Create a Race of Thoroughbreds."* [2] In October 1922, it carried an article entitled: *"The Rising Tide of Color Against White World Supremacy"* and in 1933, it had an article entitled: *"Eugenic Sterilisation: An Urgent Need"*, written by Ernst Rudin, then Hitler's director of genetic sterilization who helped establish the so-called Nazi Society for Racial Hygiene. [3]

Sanger swiftly distanced herself and her followers from any association with members of the Third Reich after the horrors of the concentration camps emerged for the world's attention. However her views remained the same.

On Men and Families

On men she wrote:

> *"47.3% of drafted men have the mentality of 12 year old children – in other words they are morons. Assuming that these drafted men are a fair sample of the population...this means nearly one-half of the entire population will never develop mental capacity beyond the state of moron... Our failure to segregate morons who are increasing and multiplying, though in truth I have merely scratched the surface of this international menace."* [4]

On large families she wrote:

> *"The most merciful thing a large family can do to one of its infant members is to kill it."* [5]

On marriage she wrote:

> *"The marriage bed is the most degenerative influence in the social order..."* [6]

---

[1] letter to Dr Clarence Gamble, 19 December 1939. original source Sophia Smith Collection, Smith College, North Hampton, Massachusetts, quoted in Grant, p40

[2] cf Marshall & Donovan p9

[3] cf Grant p39

[4] cf Drogin p64-65

[5] cf Grant p77

[6] Margaret Sanger (editor). *The Woman Rebel*, Volume I, Number 1. Reprinted in *Woman and the New Race*. New York: Brentanos Publishers, 1922

Undermining Christianity

On Christianity Sanger wrote:

> *"Birth control appeals to the advanced radical because it is calculated to undermine the authority of the Christian Churches. I look forward to seeing humanity free someday of the tyranny of Christianity..."*[1]

This quote strikingly illustrates Sanger's view on the role of contraception as a tool to undermine Christianity.

Having access to immense amounts of money from her marriages, Sanger embarked on a worldwide mission with militant, evangelistic zeal to promote what she termed her 'religion' of birth control through international conferences and meetings.

She made an enormous impact in political, media, medical, academic, religious and social policy circles worldwide, invoking the fear of political and economic disaster if the 'unfit' masses were allowed to 'spawn' and 'swarm'.

Her financial backing and direct involvement was a major factor in the development of 'the pill' in its earliest form by scientist Gregory Pincus in the 1950's.[2]

The Roots of Contraception

Modern day contraception promotion is rooted in Margaret Sanger's racist, eugenic, elitist, class discriminatory and anti-religion ideology, an ideology that most contraceptive users are unaware of.

Her work culminated in the establishment of International Planned Parenthood Federation (IPPF) in 1952, with Sanger herself as joint President.[3]

Today, IPPF is one of the world's foremost advocates of contraception, abortion, sterilization, sex education and population control. Family Planning Associations in 192 countries are members of IPPF and carry on their aims locally.

Faye Wattleton, president of Planned Parenthood of America Federation in the 1980s stated how "proud" she was to be "walking in the footsteps" of Margaret Sanger.[4] In 1991, Alexander Sanger, Margaret Sanger's grandson, became president of the New York affiliate of Planned Parenthood.[5] He was quoted:

> *"I intend to be out there on the front lines of our issues... With all her success, my grandmother left some unfinished business, and I intend to finish it."* [6]

---

[1] cf Grant p78

[2] cf Marshall &Donovan p212; cf Grant p96

[3] IPPF Fact Sheet; *A History of IPPF in the World Family Planning Movement*, March 1979

[4] Wattleton, Faye, "Humanist of the Year Acceptance Speech", *The Humanist*, July-August 1986, quoted in Grant p77

[5] cf Grant p77

[6] Another Sanger leads Planned Parenthood', *The New York Times*, January 23, 1991, pB2

The Anglican Church

In 1920, the Anglican Bishops of the Church of England stated:

> *"We utter an emphatic warning against the use of unnatural means for the avoidance of conception."* [1]

On August 14th 1930 however, the Anglican Bishops broke with the traditional teaching and opened the door to contraceptive methods in marriage in certain circumstances. Whilst the ruling initially met with a barrage of criticism and condemnation from a wide range of Protestant sources, the centuries-old consensus had been broken. Even the mainline media condemned it.

Pope Pius XI was swift in stating the Catholic Church's position:

> *"...the Catholic Church, to whom God has entrusted the defense of the integrity and purity of morals, standing erect in the midst of the moral ruin which surrounds her, in order that she may preserve the chastity of the nuptial union from being defiled by this foul stain, raises her voice in token of her divine ambassadorship and through our mouth proclaims anew: any use whatsoever of matrimony exercised in such a way that the act is deliberately frustrated in its natural power to generate life is an offense against the law of God and of nature, and those who indulge in such are branded with the guilt of a grave sin."* [2]

In time virtually all the other Protestant denominations followed suit in allowing contraception for their members. There followed an explosion of sexual promiscuity of every type now so apparent all around us today. Only the Catholic Church has remained consistent in condemning contraception, publishing several teaching documents (encyclicals) and letters on the subject since the 1930's and right up to the present day.

---

[1] Lambeth Conference 1920, Resolution 68, cited in Kippley, J. *Birth Control and Christian Discipline*, 2nd Ed, 1994, p3
[2] Pius XI, *Casti Connubii*, n56, 31 Dec 1930

Chapter Five

Protestant Views
Opposing Contraception

"For too long birth control has been looked upon as a "Catholic issue". It is fast becoming a "Protestant issue" however, as Protestant ministers like myself protest the heretical teaching of birth control that is being propagated in Protestant churches."

Rev. Matthew Trewella

Protestant Leaders Condemned Contraception

Contrary to popular belief, all the mainline Christian denominations, Protestant and Catholic, opposed contraception right up to the Anglican Bishop's conference in Lambeth in 1930. It was not just a Catholic issue.

The Protestant denominations took a Biblical basis for condemnation of contraceptive practices from the so-called 'Onan incident' of Genesis 38. In this passage, Onan is slain by God for practising what is called today "coitus interruptus" or "withdrawal". That Onan deliberately allowed his "seed" to fall to the ground has been regarded by Catholic and Protestant scholars for centuries as the central reason he incurred God's retribution. Martin Luther (1483-1546) called Onan's action:

"a most disgraceful sin. It is far more atrocious than incest or adultery." [1]

John Calvin (1509-1564), father of Calvinism, stated that Onan's action was:

"...doubly monstrous – For this is to extinguish the hope of the race and to kill before he is born the hoped - for offspring." [2]

John Wesley (1703-1791), founder of the Methodists, wrote that such practice involved the serious risk of the loss of one's soul.[3]

Charles Provan, an evangelical Lutheran who conducted extensive study on the historical Christian position on contraception over the centuries, stated:

---

[1] Provan p81
[2] Provan p68
[3] cf Provan p91

"We have found not one orthodox theologian to defend birth control before the 1900's. NOT ONE. On the other hand, we have found many highly regarded Protestant theologians were enthusiastically opposed to it, all the way back to the very beginning of the Reformation." [1]

A Modern Day View

In their book, *Open Embrace: A Protestant Couple Rethinks Contraception*, Sam and Bethany Torode argue that all married couples, not just Roman Catholics, need to seriously examine the widespread use of contraception. [2]

Explaining his frustration about the lack of understanding on this subject when he became engaged, Sam Torode writes:

> *"I wanted to think through the whole issue of birth control, so I consulted my married evangelical friends. To a person, they all said, 'Sure, of course we use birth control.' When I asked them why, bringing up the concerns other Christians have, many of them answered, 'You know, I never thought about that!'"*

The Torodes explain:

> *"As we researched the existing Christian literature on birth control, we hoped to find a book that we could hand on to people... Because we couldn't find such a book, we decided to write one. Whether you agree or disagree with the conclusions we present in Open Embrace, we hope it will challenge and encourage you, and help sharpen your moral discernment.* [3]

A Protestant Examines 'the pill'

Many people are shocked to discover that the contraceptive pill can cause abortion of newly conceived human beings, a subject discussed in Chapter Six. On this subject, author and evangelical pastor Randy Alcorn has written a meticulous book *"Does the Birth Control Pill cause Abortions?"* [4]

Exhaustively researched and citing the most up to date medical literature, Rev. Alcorn's book provides a compelling argument why Christians should not use chemical

> *"We have found not one orthodox theologian to defend Birth Control before the 1900's. NOT ONE"*
>
> Charles Provan

---

[1] Provan p63

[2] cf Torode

[3] Torode, S & B, *Open Embrace, Christians rethinking* Contraception cf http://www.lifeissues.net/writers/tor/tor_02rethinkingcontra.html ; www.torodedesign.com/NEW/why.html 2004

[4] Alcorn, R., *Does the Birth Control Pill cause abortions?* Eternal Perspectives Ministries, 6th edition, 2002

contraceptive methods. Its primary aim is to expose the abortion-causing potential of the commonly known 'pill', Norplant, Depo-Provera, intra-uterine devices and other products. While it does not condemn all contraception, the book is of great help for Christians taking a first step away from chemical contraception with abortion-causing potential. It can be obtained from the website www.epm.org.

Vasectomy Reversed

Going one step further, Protestant Minister Rev. Matthew Trewella outlines the biblical basis why birth control opposes scripture. In his article: *The Protest of a Protestant Minister Against Birth Control*, Rev. Trewella outlines his throes of fear and apprehension, and ultimately the reasons why he chose to have his vasectomy reversed.[1]

Rev. Trewella comments:

> *"For too long birth control has been looked upon as a "Catholic issue". It is fast becoming a "Protestant issue" however, as Protestant ministers like myself protest the heretical teaching of birth control that is being propagated in Protestant churches.*
>
> *We must understand that the Church, whether Catholic, Protestant or Orthodox, spoke consistently for 1900 years against birth control. Only in the last 75 years have Protestant churches begun to peddle this belief that God thinks it's okay or wise for us to use birth control."* [2]

Rev. Trewella's organization *Protestants Against Birth Control*, has a leaflet entitled *Everything you Never wanted to know about Birth Control – A Guide for Engaged and Newlywed Couples*.[3] Again dealing with the abortion-causing potential of the 'pill', Norplant, intra-uterine devices and others, the final sentence concludes:

> *"We invite you to join us in the conviction that children are among the most wonderful blessings and gifts in the world. We believe that God can plan our families infinitely better than we ever could!"*

"Protestant ministers like myself protest the heretical teaching of birth control that is being propagated in Protestant churches."

Rev. Matthew Trewella

---

[1] Trewella, Rev M., "The Protest of a Protestant Minister Against Birth Control", Leaflet, Mercy Seat Christian Church, Milwaukee, Wisconsin, USA, www.missionariestopreborn.com

[2] www.missionariestopreborn.com/birth_control.html

[3] Protestants Against Birth Control, P.O. Box 26931, Milwaukee, WI 53266, USA, see web address above

In his commentary, 'The Blight of Birth Control; its anti-scriptural bias', Lutheran Walter Arthur Maier wrote:

> "In spite of extended argument, not a single passage can be adduced from scripture which even in any remote way condones birth control; and no one even acquainted with the Bible should hesitate to admit that it is a definite departure from the requirements of Scripture. See Gen 38:9,10." [1]

The evidence outlined above is not an exhaustive study of Protestant thinking opposing birth control. It does however provide enough basis for Protestant believers (who do not regard themselves compelled to comply with Catholic Church teaching) to seriously question the role of birth control and how it affects marriage, family, the sanctity of life and obedience to God's plan. [2]

New Protestant Websites

Evangelical Christian Internet sites such as www.quiverfull.com advocate large families based on Psalm 127:5:

> "Lo. Children are a heritage of the Lord: and the fruit of the womb is His reward. Happy is the man that hath his quiver full of them."

This website's homepage declares how:

×   its members exalt Jesus Christ as Lord,
×   that they acknowledge His headship in their lives, including fertility,
×   they exist to serve those believers who trust the Lord to determine their family size, and
×   to answer the questions of those seeking the truth in this critical area of marriage

Brimming with resources and articles, it is typical of new Christian websites offering a fresh Protestant view on contraception.

Author's note: The author does not necessarily agree with or endorse all the views expressed in the websites or sources cited above. They are cited with the sole purpose of representing a range of views opposing contraception amongst Protestant thinkers.

---

[1] cf Provan, p81-82

[2] Another interesting article by Allan Carlson is "Children of the Reformation – A Short and Surprising History of Protestantism and Contraception" *Touchstone Magazine* May 2007

Chapter Six

The Abortifacient Nature of Contraceptive Drugs

"I listened in horror as I learnt it is possible to conceive and then lose a child by early abortion while using the pill."

A wife

Many Contraceptives are Abortifacient

Before examining the principal tenet of this book, there is one crucial issue every woman should know.

As a pharmacist I know that nearly all the contraceptive pills, intra-uterine devices, depot injections and chemical preparations have an abortifacient (abortion causing) action as part of their overall mechanism.[1] This action is admitted by pill manufacturers albeit couched in technical, pharmacological language.[2] This means that women can unknowingly abort their own child just after conception on any given month during contraceptive use. How many women realise that?

In my experience as a pharmacist, many women are horrified when they realise they may be aborting their own children by using the pill or other products. "Why didn't anyone tell us?" they ask.

The abortion-causing nature of the pill was the clinching factor in 1993 in my ceasing to dispense contraceptive drugs as a pharmacist, even though it meant subsequent unemployment for three years in my profession. This abortion causing effect of contraceptives is examined more closely in my first book *Contraception and Evangelium Vitae.*

How does the pill cause abortion? Let's take a closer look.

Fertilisation

Each month a woman's ovary releases an egg (ovum). This process is called ovulation. See diagram on next page outlining the process of human conception.

The ovum slowly travels down the fallopian tubes towards the womb (uterus). If intercourse has taken place the sperm enter the vagina and make their way through the cervix, into the uterus and up to the fallopian tube where only one may fertilise the ovum.

---

[1] See appendix 2; *Do Contraceptive Pills cause Abortions?*
[2] For Appendix 2 for a direct quotation for pill product 'Femodene'.

One sperm fuses with the ovum in a process called conception (fertilisation). At this point a new unique human being has been created.

This single cell begins to divide and sub-divide (embryo) and contains the complex genetic blueprint for every detail of this new human person's development... the child's sex, hair and eye colour, height etc.

The embryo then travels down the fallopian tube towards the uterus – a journey that takes about four days.

Meanwhile the lining of the uterus (endometrium) is being prepared so that that implantation of the embryo in the wall of the uterus can take place. Implantation usually occurs five to seven days following conception.

Following a period of nine months gestation, a fully developed baby is ready to be born.

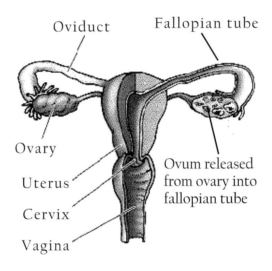

The Process of
Human Conception

The pill and other contraceptive drugs effect their contraceptive action by causing the inner lining of the mother's womb to be hostile, or unreceptive, to implantation by the newly conceived human life. The newly conceived life is denied development and will die and pass out, perhaps unnoticed by its mother.

As detailed in Appendix 2, ovulation can occur from 0% to 60% of 'break-through' cycles depending on the type of pill used. The abortifacient mechanism is thus enabled should conception occur during any of these break-through cycles.

Recently one woman wrote to me:

> "I got married at 35 and we tried for a family from the start. In the first year of marriage we attended one of your talks on the abortifacient (abortion-causing)

nature of the contraceptive pill. I listened in horror as I learnt it is possible to conceive and then lose a child by early abortion while using the pill. I was in shock and remained in shock for quite a few years. Sometimes I think I am still in shock when I ponder on that fact alone.

How many years I lived in the "culture of death". In effect I may well have caused my children to die when I took the contraceptive pill and engaged in premarital sexual activity. The thought of one day meeting Jesus and hearing Him say to me "these are the children you aborted though your use of the contraceptive pill" was very distressing.

But God's grace and infinite mercy can and does bring healing. I deeply regretted the fact I hadn't made more of an effort to inform my conscience, but in my teenage years and twenties I didn't seem to have the inclination to do so." [1]

Quite a few women have feelings of remorse and grief with the dawning realisation of what may have happened. Another woman wrote of her contraceptive pill use:

"For the first time in my life, I came to grips with the fact that I had not only shut myself off to life, but had also destroyed an unknown number of children. As I came out of that exhibit (The Wonder of Life) there was a giant rushing water fountain nearby. I walked over to it and began to sob uncontrollably. I stayed there for some time, absorbed in my sudden feelings of grief and remorse. This was the very first time I became aware of the full impact of what I had done. I am here to say that I will be 'Silent No More' about the children that I aborted through birth control." [2]

This woman went on to describe the subsequent healing of her 'post-abortion' grief. She co-founded an organisation to help women to come to terms with similar experiences. [3]

What then about all the lives cut short by the abortifacient nature of the pill and other so-called contraceptives causing the death of children just after conception? [4]

> "I am here to say that I will be 'Silent No More' about the children that I aborted through birth control."
>
> Former contraceptive user

---

[1] SE, Personal communication 22 August 2007

[2] cf Burke, T p17-18

[3] cf www.silentnomoreawareness.org and www.rachelsvineyard.org

[4] cf appendix 2

63

Chapter Seven

The Catholic Church
and Procreation

*The Catholic Church... regards itself as
messenger and proclaimer of Christ's
liberating Gospel, not as dictator or killjoy.*

Cornerstone Teaching

Let's be clear here. There is a statement - it is claimed - that reflects God's will that, if true, has enormous repercussions for married couples and even the entire world.

This statement has caused enormous controversy, vociferous objection and misunderstanding since it was formally articulated in 1968. It is deceptively simple, but its implications are profound. It has the power to *utterly transform* a marriage depending on how seriously it is taken. It is a statement that, with the test of time, doesn't go away. It is this:

"...each and every marriage act must be open to the transmission of life." [1]

These words, written by Pope Paul VI in his encyclical *Humanae Vitae*, state that, in God's plan, every act of sexual intercourse ever undertaken between husband and wife throughout their entire married lives must remain open to the possibility that it could result in the conception of a child.

The marital act, according to *Humanae Vitae*, has two dimensions that are inseparable: the union of spouses and procreation. [2] In other words, contraception can have no part in marriage.

Obedience Means Life

Our son Francis, when he was four, was almost killed by a car one day when out with his mum and sisters. They were crossing the road when suddenly a car appeared out of a 'blind spot' from behind another vehicle. My wife screamed: "Francis STOP" to Francis, who hadn't seen the car. At that instant,

> *"...each and every marriage act must be open to the transmission of life"*
>
> HV n11

---

[1] HVn11
[2] cfHVn12

four years of discipline and instruction to obey mum and dad stopped him in his tracks, and the car sped past. At that critical moment Francis's life depended entirely on his obedience to his mother. He obeyed – and lived.

This story illustrates a crucial principle of human existence - 'obedience means life'. More specifically, obedience to *God's will* means life... including eternal life.

When the Church teaches 'No' or 'Stop' in its moral teaching, its not being a kill-joy or trying to thwart our freedom. It is saving us from harm and bringing us life.

An inescapable truth for every person, and especially for every Christian, is found in the comment:

> *"Man cannot attain that true happiness for which he yearns... unless he keeps the laws which the Most High God has engraved in his very nature."* [1]

In other words, it is obedience to God's will and laws which brings peace and 'life to the full'. God does not expect the obedience of slaves who obey out of fear, nor the obedience of employees who obey out of hope of a reward. He calls us to the obedience of sons and daughters who obey out of love and respect for their heavenly Father.

Every Christian, every Catholic, has a duty to *obedience*. A tough word, but a liberating one if properly understood. The Psalmist notes:

> *"Happy the man who fears the Lord,*
> *who takes delight in all his commands."* [2]

Interestingly, these words are immediately followed by a promise of the welfare of one's children:

> *"His sons will be powerful on earth*
> *The children of the upright are blessed."*[3]

IF it is true that God wants EVERY marital act to be 'open to life' (that is, not closed to life by contraception), then it is only marital intercourse that is open to life which will facilitate true marital fulfilment and happiness.

Our choices relating to birth control and the procreation and spacing of our children will profoundly affect the measure of our achievements over our lifetime.

> *Every Christian, every Catholic, has a duty to obedience. A tough word, but a liberating one if properly understood*

---

[1] cf HV n31

[2] Ps111 (112) v1

[3] v2

To Contracept or Not to Contracept?

The pharmaceutical companies, birth control agencies, family planning organisations and others with massive, vested financial interests and hugely persuasive marketing efforts are clear in what decision *they* want *you* to make.

Each of us has to make a decision regarding contraception. The mission of the Catholic Church is to bring the whole of mankind to salvation in Jesus Christ. In this sense, it is a servant of the people of God and the whole world.

The Church believes it has been divinely appointed by Christ as the authentic guardian, interpreter and teacher of God's truth and laws. It has a lot to say on the subject of marriage, procreation and the planning of births.[**]

The Church regards itself as a messenger of Christ's liberating Gospel. As is clear in *Humanae Vitae*, it regards itself as 'interpreter' and 'depository' of His teaching, not its author.[1]

Most people who disagree with the Church's teaching haven't, in my experience, read *Humanae Vitae* let alone the other writings of the Catholic Church on this subject. Many such folk don't coherently know what the Church teaches. How then can they credibly reject it?

[**] The key texts of the Catholic Church on this subject include *Humanae Vitae* (Of Human Life) Pope Paul VI 1968, *Gaudium et Spes* (On the Church in the Modern World) 1965 Pope Paul VI , *Letter to Families* 1994, Pope John Paul II, *Casti Connubii* (On Christian Marriage) 1930 Pope Pius XI, *Familiaris Consortio* (Christian Family in the Modern World) 1981 Pope John Paul II, *Theology of the Body* series of addresses 1979-1981 Pope John Paul II, *Vademecum to Confessors* 1997 Pontifical Council for the Family, *Evangelium Vitae* (The Gospel of Life) 1995 Pope John Paul II, *Donum Vitae* (The Gift of Life) 1987 Congregation For the Doctrine of the Faith, *Catechism of the Catholic Church* 1997 2nd edition, *Love and Responsibility* 1993 revised edition Karol Wojtyla, later Pope John Paul II, and *Mulieris Dignatem* (On the Dignity of Women) 1998 Pope John Paul II. Quotations from these documents and sources are included in this book.

[1] Cf HV n 18

Chapter Eight

Contraception
A Potent Destroyer of Marriage

"During this time I felt really low, really cheap. There was no communication, no hugging. It was all about physical gratification. It wasn't love; it was horrible."

Mary, wife

A Young Couple's Story

Tom and Mary*, a young married Catholic couple from Northern Ireland, always believed contraception was wrong. However, through a culmination of misfortunes, family difficulties, financial pressures, long working hours, isolation from friends and the tragic loss of a preborn child, they resorted to contraception.

Here is their experience:

TOM: "Our child dying was the final nail. It killed my faith in God. We turned to contraception... Our sexual relationship changed from an act of marital union to a lust-filled activity. I no longer saw my wife as a person – I lost respect for her – I started looking at other women – I saw pornography as OK – I saw it as helping my love life."

MARY: "During that time I felt really low, really cheap. There was no communication, no hugging. It was all about physical gratification. It wasn't love; it was horrible. My self-confidence plummeted. When we started using contraception, a lot changed, even our personalities. I started to feel bad towards Tom; I could see him change and I didn't like the person he was becoming. I knew how he felt about me. I became horrible to him. We had a lot of arguments and our marriage became emotional and aggressive."

TOM: "I found myself thinking about other women during our love-making – Mary wasn't even 'there'. I knew she wasn't enjoying it but I didn't care. The act was becoming boring, so you start to explore other ways for more pleasure. It was over very quickly – Mary was left there not feeling good. I was satisfied and that was the main thing. We had five healthy children, I

---

* Names have been changed for personal reasons

just wanted the pleasure and no hassle. Condoms were awkward, so – on bad advice - I signed up for a vasectomy."

MARY: "The rot started in the intimate area of our marriage and spread into other areas. For me, it was the use of contraception that killed off my faith. At one point, I thought our marriage couldn't last. I knew he didn't care for me and I was falling out of love with him. Most women want affection and there was none. I remember really wanting some affection. I began to think of getting it with 'someone else'. We were two horrible people to be with. We both started to think of separation. But I so wanted to save our marriage."

TOM: "The sin was blinding me. I didn't want to see it. I stopped caring, got lazy, watched a lot of material on TV that I shouldn't have. I bought sleazy newspapers – I didn't think anything was wrong with it. I was listening to all this bravado man-talk at work and coming home to play it out at night. For the first time I started to feel free from the 'binds' of Catholicism. There was no communication between us."

MARY: "I started to think of how happier we were in our earlier days when we had tried NFP. I thought contraception was bringing us misfortune. I cried out to God for help. 'We can't live like this any longer. We need support. We need friends.' I broke down and wept."

This stark, sad experience of Tom and Mary thankfully had a *dramatic turnaround* as we will see later. Could it be that their bruising experience of imminent marital disintegration through contraceptive use has something to say to every married couple?

The 'Person' Becomes an 'Object' of Pleasure

In Tom and Mary's own words, their love changed to lust; the husband focused on his own pleasure; the wife relates how she felt low and cheap; they both felt cut off from God. He was soon to get a vasectomy. Break-up was staring them in the face... unification was ebbing away and the pursuit of pleasure was taking centre stage.

In contraception or sterilisation, when the procreative power is removed, something fundamentally changes in the nature of the relationship.[1] The 'total' and 'self-giving' elements of marital love are no longer there.

Contraception propagates 'self' rather than the 'other'. It causes users to seek self-orientated pleasure rather than the 'good' of the other. The focus

> When the procreative power is removed, something fundamentally changes in the nature of the relationship.

---

[1] cf LRp228

tends to move from the good of the 'other' person to 'my' pleasure. Man and woman begin to mutually use each other.[1] Another woman wrote:

> "After my tubes were tied, I felt so empty. Lovemaking with my husband became purposeless and lost its meaning. Our marriage bed was no longer holy or sacred, but...hedonistic. We were both becoming self-absorbed in our own orgasms. Our bedroom relationship wasn't very loving." [2]

In such a scenario, there is a 'debasement of the human body'.[3] The spouses and their sexuality are degraded and manipulated.[4]

Gerard and Marie's Story

Now consider the real life experience of Gerard and Marie, a husband and wife in Ireland, who started using the pill and found their marriage starting to deteriorate:

GERARD: "We had three pregnancies in eighteen months! "Hold on!" I said. " This has to stop!"

MARIE: "There were endless nappies and finances were very tight. When we went on the contraceptive pill, we were delirious with delight. Pure unabated freedom!! No responsibility! We embarked on a new intoxicating liberty. It was fabulous. We could turn our fertility on and off. Then we had another child – now we had the 'perfect' family - two boys, two girls. WE were in control."

GERARD: "But after a couple of years, things had definitely changed. I'd grown bored with all this intercourse. I no longer desired or looked forward to it. From one month to the next, I didn't care whether it happened or not. My wife was using the pill all through this time."

MARIE: "My husband would get into bed at night to read and I'd lie there feeling rejected. He'd say to me: "maybe tomorrow night". The fact you could have intercourse every night meant it lost its specialness."

GERARD: "I was thinking to myself; 'Something is amiss here. But I wouldn't speak about it. I was afraid to face up to it in case it made things worse. There was a widening rift – a breakdown in communication – but I wouldn't talk about it. I thought this was only a phase and that it would pass. I loved my wife and I knew she loved me. But it didn't pass. At this time there was a serious temptation to think about other women during our intimate moments. Looking back at that time, I now realise how easy it is to fall into that trap during contraceptive use."

---

[1] cf LFn13; cf LRp228
[2] cf Burke, T p36
[3] Deus Caritas Est n5
[4] cf FCn32

MARIE: "There was this sense of looking for fulfilment elsewhere. We were developing different interests. The intimate part of our marriage seemed to be dying. As parents we were still completely involved, but we each were swift to agree to activities outside the home...committees, night classes, sport. We didn't feel important to one another anymore.

Then one night at a meeting a woman said: *"Contraception puts a barrier between you and your husband and between you and God."* That hit a chord. There was a barrier between us. I knew it was true. We went to a married couples retreat weekend called Marriage Encounter. As a result, I went to the sacrament of confession and I was crying my eyes out with relief. There was such a sense of freedom in receiving absolution from the priest..." (Story completed later)

> *"The intimate part of our marriage seemed to be dying... we didn't feel important to one another anymore."*
>
> Marie, wife

A Growing Rift

Gerard and Marie's experience of the effect of contraception on their marriage could be repeated for so many couples.

Boredom, breakdown in communication, the loss of sense of specialness to each other, the feeling of separation from each other, a sense of separation from God and the temptation to look elsewhere for fulfilment – these are classical symptoms repeatedly cited by couples turning to contraception.[1]

A Psychotherapist Speaks

In his professional experience of counselling hundreds of married couples, medical doctor and psychotherapist Dr. Bob McDonald has discovered that contraception, or sterilisation, lies at the root of a huge range of marital problems. He makes a revealing and striking statement:

> *"Disintegration of the sexual intimacy between a husband and wife is the first and most obvious sign of disorder for a contracepting couple."* [2]

Here is what Dr. McDonald states can typically occur in a marriage that uses contraception;

× After starting contraception, the focus for a husband typically becomes increasingly centred on pursuing his own sensation of pleasure, and less and less on his wife's experience.

---

[1] cf Burke, T ; cf Shivanandan Chapter 8
[2] cf McDonald

- Spouses, especially the wives, increasingly become sexual objects. She has to meet her husband's desires when he wants them satisfied. This is the message that is communicated to wives.

- As the focus becomes more and more on his personal satisfaction, legitimate intercourse becomes less and less satisfying.

- The husband then starts to seek more heightened pleasure in distorted sexual practices with his wife.

- As things progress, the husband needs ever-increasing stimulation to achieve the pleasure he had at the beginning. He starts looking for even more sources of stimulation; X-rated videos, pornography on the internet, magazines etc. (Dr. McDonald cites that 3% of internet sites are pornographic, and these 3% of sites account for 80% of all internet hits).

- Ultimately, this leads to loss of pleasure of true conjugal union. Instead it is replaced by an insatiable erotic desire which medical practitioners term 'sexual addiction'.

- The spouses become alienated. The wife is no longer regarded as a gift and co-equal. Instead she has become an object of lust to meet her husband's demands.

- The wife begins to realise that she is being used. She realises she has been cooperating in the destruction of her feminine essence... that openness to new life which is built into her being. At this stage, Dr. McDonald reports, many women begin to struggle with a sense of frustrated maternity, especially where the husband is determined not to have children.

- She typically becomes depressed. If she mentions having children, he gets angry. He sees her as going back on their initial agreement not to have children and he doesn't like it.

- The scene is set for irritability, resentment, rage, discord and breakdown.

- Tragically, one or the other may enter an adulterous relationship, the ultimate betrayal of the marriage covenant.

Dr. McDonald's observations about the impact of contraception on marriage are certainly borne out by the experience of other couples. Dr. McDonald's experience reflects that of other health care professionals working in this field. For example, Dr. Dominic Pedulla, from his work, raises the prospect that contraception is one of the most important, overlooked factors in a host of medical, emotional and social conditions afflicting modern women.[1]

---

[1] cf www.the-edith-stein-foundation.com

Loss of Respect for Women
A Side-Effect of Contraception

The testimonies in this book reveal that wives feel used and disrespected in a contraceptive marriage.

Consider the following words of Pope Paul VI:

> "It is also to be feared that the man, growing used to the employment of anticonceptive practices, may finally lose respect for the woman and, no longer caring for her physical and psychological equilibrium, may come to the point of considering her as a mere instrument of selfish enjoyment, and no longer as his respected and beloved companion." [1]

These words were written in 1968. Yet they are so relevant today. If the pill manufacturers were legally required to cite the selfish abuse of women by men as a possible side-effect of the pill, would it be as popular?

Contraception-Disintegration of Sexual Harmony

In the words of Dr. McDonald, disintegration of the sexual intimacy between a husband and wife is *"the first and most obvious sign of disorder for a contracepting couple."* Why is this so?

Amongst those known to me whose marriages have broken up or have had serious marital difficulties ALL of them had used contraception. It is a key component to identify for any couple whose marriage is struggling. There is always hope of improvement in any struggling marriage but in these situations, clear steps must be taken to stop contraception. This is an area that merits

Why is it that *removing procreation from the marital act* appears to have such a damaging effect on marriage?

In short why does it seem that contraception is a potent contributory factor in marriage break-up?

Read on.

There is always hope for improvement in any struggling marriage...

---

[1] HVn17

Chapter Nine

What Happens During Contraception?
- The Destruction of Love, Intimacy, Life

True conjugal love unites, contraception separates,
and the separation works right down the line.
It not only separates sex from procreation,
it also separates sex from love. It separates pleasure from
meaning, and body from mind. Ultimately and surely, it
separates wife from husband and husband from wife."

Mgr C. Burke, Author
'Covenanted Happiness –
Love and Commitment in Marriage'

Union and Procreation Separated

With contraception, the bonds which hold marriage together are dissolved.

As outlined in Figure 1 on the next page, with contraception, intercourse between spouses is separated from the power to conceive a child. Union and procreation are separated.

Once intercourse is separated from procreation, the sexual act becomes an end in itself. Once the sexual act is removed from marriage, any expression of the act becomes possible.

When contraception is introduced into a marriage, the spouses can start to feel they are drifting apart.

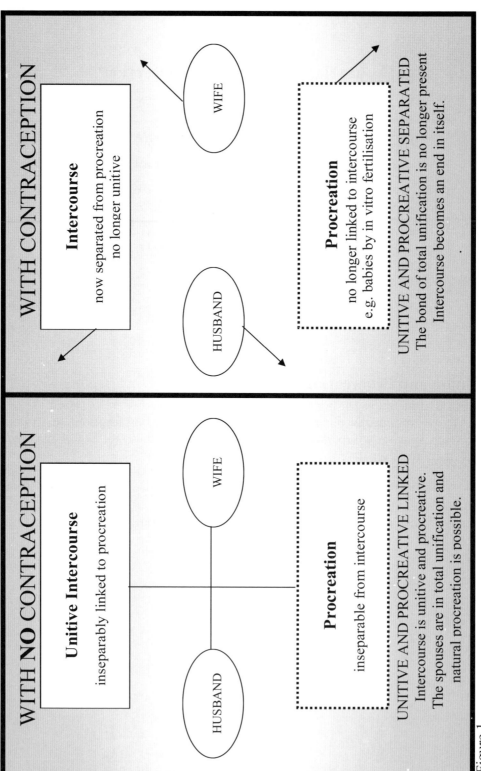

Figure 1

Contraception Affects Union

Gerard and Marie felt a loss of union in their marriage when they used contraception. They were drifting apart. There was a barrier between them. That sense of true union, in mind and heart, started to slip away.

When the procreation of children is severed from marital intercourse, something changes at the very deepest level of the relationship. In contraception, there is no true union of persons. That is because the gift of fertility, which is 'part of the human person'[1] is withheld from each spouse.

A marital act open to life says: "I am willing to have with you a permanent commitment and new life, should it occur. I respect you." Contraceptive intercourse says (even though couples may not realise it): 'I am willing for now, for my pleasure, but I don't want all of you and don't tie me in too much..."

Some Statistical Evidence

An interesting correlation between the use of contraception and divorce rates is highlighted in research by social scientist Robert T Michael.[2]

In his statistical analysis of divorce rates in the USA from 1930 to 1983, Michael correlates 50% of the rise in divorce rates between 1962-1974 to the greater availability and efficacy of contraception.

With 73% of married women aged 15-49 years in the USA using some form of contraception (36,000,000 women approx), there is a current divorce / separation rate of 43%-50% for people presently getting married in the USA.[3]

In contrast, markedly lower divorce rates (0.2% - 5%) are reported amongst users of natural family planning. (NFP). [4]

Contraception Separates

The separating effect of contraception in marriage was observed by Rev. Cormac Burke from his experience of working with married couples:

> *"True conjugal love unites, contraception separates, and the separation works right down the line. It not only separates sex from procreation, it also separates sex from love. It separates pleasure from meaning, and body from mind. Ultimately and surely, it separates wife from husband and husband from wife."* [5]

---

[1] cf HV n10

[2] cf Michael

[3] cf www.unstats.un.org Kreider, Rose M., Fields, Jason M, Number, Timing and Duration of Marriages and Divorces, Fall 1996; U.S. Census Bureau, *Current Population Reports* p70-80, 2001, Washington DC, www.census.gov - 2002 publications; National Center for Health Statistics, Hyattsville, MD 20782, www.cdc.gov/nchs; cf www.divorcereform.org

[4] cf Wilson; cf Couple to Couple League, 4290 Delhi Pike, Cincinnati, Ohio, USA 45238, see website www.ccli.org ; cf de Stoop p63; cf Wetzel, R., M.D. *Sexual Wisdom. A Guide for Parents. Young Adults, Educators and Physicians*, Proctor Publications, 1998, cf p114

[5] Burke, C p38

He adds:

> "*Contraceptive couples who stop to reflect realize that their marriage is troubled by some deep malaise. The alienations they are experiencing are a sign as well as a consequence of the grave violation of the moral order involved in contraception.*"

Contraception Damages Real Communication

A wife writes about contraceptive use:

> "*My deepest needs as a woman were not being fulfilled. I craved intimacy, love, tenderness and communication. My husband spent years thinking he was the best lover in the world. He never realised (until we started using natural family planning), that I never felt loved by him as long as he was willing to use me whenever the urge hit him... It grieves me that we spent so many years trying to figure it out, fumbling through urges and temptations, seeking any methods available for instant gratification. Trying to please my husband and be desirable left me with feelings of resentment and bitterness. No one talks about these deep cravings.*" [1]

As Gerard and Marie experienced, with contraception, real communication tends to break down. Tom and Mary said it. The lady quoted above indicated it. Intimacy dissipates in many couple's experience. When the procreative capacity of the marital act is removed, something changes in the relationship. The intimacy is thrown out of kilter. Spouses 'view' each other differently, and for many couples true communication ceases.

Will Every Contracepting Couple Break Up?

Not every couple who contracept will have a marital breakdown. However, the introduction of contraception into a marriage radically changes the nature of the marriage at a fundamental level. It is as if a vital defence is stripped away. It appears some marriages are more vulnerable to the effects of contraception than others.

But in every marriage, the marital love between spouses and even the way they regard each other, is altered when contraception is used. Couples relate how contraception opens a door through which a niggling, unsettling doubt can enter.

Contraception is a 'Lie'

Would you lie to someone you love? Would you like the person you love to lie to you? As Pope John Paul II notes, with contraception or sterilisation the meaning of the marital act is falsified. The act becomes as a 'lie'. [2]

---

[1] cf Burke, T p44
[2] cf FCn11, cfFCn32

This is because the body goes through the 'motions' of total self-giving, but *total self-giving is no longer present*. There is serious reservation. There is no longer a total self-giving of the whole person when fertility is denied. One husband who had a vasectomy wrote:

> *"We no longer had to worry about pregnancy or about the negative health effects of the pill. We could now enjoy sex "any time, any place". We were in control of our sexuality, and free from any daily birth control, or so I thought. The reality of the situation was that our sex life didn't get any better. In fact, it was probably starting to diminish... Our time in the bedroom was spent going through the motions without any real purpose."*[1]

Through the falsification entailed with contraception, the marital act becomes "*intrinsically dishonest.*"[2] In other words it becomes a lie. Its real purpose is radically compromised and even lost completely and it is no longer a true renewal of the couple's love. If such an act is truly dishonest, how can this be good for a marriage?

Can such dishonesty be good for a marriage?

The Marital Act Ceases to be an Act of Love

In what may be perceived as a stark statement in today's modern culture, Pope John Paul II points out that an act of marital intercourse using contraception actually **ceases to be an act of love**:

> *"...the conjugal act, deprived of its interior truth because it is artificially deprived of its procreative capacity, ceases...to be an act of love."*[3]

The procreative capacity is an essential part of what it is to love in the marital act. During the contraceptive act, feelings of love may be present, a sensation of pleasure or desire, or a sense of fidelity or attraction to the other person may be operating. But, reflecting John Paul II's observation above, the nature of love between spouses is so radically changed that Cormac Burke notes:

> *"Love may somehow be present in their contraceptive relationship, conjugal love is not expressed by it."*[4]

Destruction of Love... The Worst Problem of All

Mother Teresa, heroine of Calcutta, had this to say about the power of contraception to destroy love:

---

[1] Burke, T p27-28 .
[2] cf HV n14
[3] cf TOB p398
[4] Burke, C p35

"In destroying the power of giving life through contraception, a husband or wife is doing something to self. This turns the attention to self and so destroys the gifts of love in him or her. In loving, the husband and wife must turn the attention to each other...many spouses do not love each other enough to practise NFP.

We cannot solve all the problems of the world, but let us never bring in the worst problem of all and that is to destroy love. And this happens when we tell people to practise contraception."[1]

Contraception Robs your Fruitfulness

Not only does it thwart the true expression of love, but contraception robs marriage of its fruitfulness, many of its blessings and the gifts of children that are bestowed on marriage by God. It denies marriage its 'crowning glory', its 'supreme gift', its 'primary blessing' and those proverbial 'arrows' in your quiver; children. It turns a marriage away from welcoming Christ when it turns away another little child. The marriage is also denied the strengthening effect another child could bring.

One day a lady who had contracepted in her marriage sadly commented to a friend of mine:

"All my married life I've always felt there was a place missing at the meal table."[2]

How Many Children Does *God* Want for *Your* Family?

I know a couple who deliberately stopped having children after their second child. The two children are beautiful, endowed with health, opportunities and material things.

But how many other 'beautiful children' might God have had in mind to send? How many other children flourishing with goodness, kindness and a desire to help in the world around them could have been born? Could that couple not have given themselves, their two children, their grandparents, their family circles, their local communities, the country, the world, the other children God wanted them to have? Perhaps one of these children was destined to care for them in their old age.

The point here is not to have as many children as possible. It is a matter of remaining open to life, exercising responsible parenthood according to one's circumstances (as elaborated in chapter fourteen) and discerning how many children *God* wants for *your* family as time unfolds.

Do a contracepting couple not deprive themselves of the real treasures they possess at the end of their lives? How can one know the future greatness of such a child whose existence was thwarted by contraception? Had they followed God's

---

[1] Mother Teresa's address to the National Prayer Breakfast, USA, Washington DC, 1998, as cited in De Stoop p57

[2] JL Personal communication 29 Nov 2005

plan for their family size, they would have arrived at the right number of children that God had in mind.

Why would anyone let themselves be sold short of even one treasure? However, as we will see in Part Three of this book, even for those who have gone down such a path, its never too late to check ourselves and begin again. As St. Paul tells us, God works all things to the good for those who love Him.[1]

Contraceptive Pill Causes Infertility

Medical evidence indicates that contraceptive pill use can cause infertility later in life.[2] One woman wrote to me:

> *"I took the contraceptive pill continuously from age 21 to 34. It seemed like the sensible thing to do, to regulate my periods, keep away period pains and to hide the fact I was sexually active. When I got married at 35, my husband and I discovered we were infertile. When we went for treatment, the doctors told me my thirteen years on the pill had more than likely been a big contributing factor to my infertility causing low cervical mucus levels and various other problems.*
>
> *I was initially angry that my doctor or someone else in my life hadn't told me pill usage could cause infertility. I now accept that my contraceptive usage is probably one of the main reasons we may never have children."* [3]

What About Children Born to a Contraceptive Marriage?

What about children already born who know mum and dad are contracepting? Will they wonder about those brothers and sisters not allowed to be born? One lady wrote:

> *"My mother encouraged me to use the pill in my teens and twenties. She used it herself in her own marriage. I wish now I'd more brothers and sisters. I feel I missed out. Now my mother herself wishes she had more grandchildren."* [4]

Another young lady told my wife she was brought up in a household of four children. For years their mother lamented frequently that she had wanted only three children instead of four. The four children grew up feeling that one of them was unwanted.

What impact does that have on children born in such a marriage? What about their sense of self-worth? "Did mum and dad not want me when I was conceived?" Fr Paul Marx, founder of Human Life International, often said that contracepting parents means contracepting teenagers.

---

[1] cf Romans 8:28
[2] see Appendix 1
[3] MM personal communication 2007
[4] Sharon M, Sept 2007

Sharon M cited above added:

> "*Mum and dad are separated and mum's quite lonely now. I've no children for her through my contraceptive-induced infertility. I can see now how contraception travels down a family from mother to daughter onwards, affecting an entire family line.*"

The effects of contraception psychologically, socially, physically, and even spiritually on children born into a contraceptive marriage is an area that needs further examination.

What Happens to Men in Contraception?
The Chivalry Factor

In an article on chivalry, author Mitchell Kalpakgian examines the concepts of chivalry and sacrifice, of courtesy and the ideals of manhood, particularly in the education of young men and in their relationships with women.

Kalpakgian writes about contraception:

> "*The most insidious underminer of chivalry, however, is contraception...A chivalrous man gives with liberality; a contracepting man... refuses the gift of total self-surrender, frustrating the fecund nature of love. A chivalrous man protects and defends women; but a contracepting man exposes a woman's health to many hazards, carelessly ignoring the many side-effects and potential dangers such as cervical cancer, liver cancer, heart attacks, strokes, depression, migraines and hair loss.*
>
> *A chivalrous man keeps his word, honors the truth, and is bound by the highest moral principles; a contracepting or sterilised man tells a lie with his body, pretending to give without really giving, and avoiding the truth that the act of love and the beginning of life are inseparable.*
>
> *A chivalrous man is thoughtful and courteous, respecting a woman's sensibilities and giving no offense in thought, word or deed; but a contracepting man lacks tact and delicacy, assuming that contraception allows constant availability and instant gratification.*
>
> *Chivalry cannot thrive in a culture dominated by the contraceptive mentality where men are wont to take and use rather than to serve, give and sacrifice.*"[1]

---

[1] Kalpakgian, M. "Chivalry Scorned is Love Denatured." *New Oxford Review* October 2000, p29-32 Vol LXVII, no. 9. Used with permission

The virtue of self-mastery wanes with contraception. People who contracept are unable or unwilling to exercise chaste self-mastery – to control their will for a greater good. Fr Paul Marx used to say "Birth control; no birth and no control".

Just how do today's contracepting men square
up in the chivalry ranks?

Fulfilment with 'Someone Else'?

When spouses use contraception, the true fulfilment of marital intercourse open to life is no longer attainable. It then becomes easier to wonder if fulfilment could be satisfied with 'someone else'. We saw that in some of the earlier testimonies.

Men in particular appear more prone to such fantasizing thoughts during contraceptive marital acts with their spouses. They are often shocked by what is going on in their minds and they know their wives would be horrified if they knew what they were thinking. One man told me:

> "When my wife went on the pill, the act started to become routine. Your mind then starts to wander into all sorts of unfaithful thoughts about other women."

Contraception Fosters an Abortion Mentality

It is often said that using contraception helps reduce surgical abortion statistics. Recently I received the following email from a lady:

> "*Twelve years of dabbling in contraceptive use – all the while exposing myself to the possibility of chemical abortion, could so easily have culminated in surgical abortion... In contraceptive intercourse you are engaging in risk-taking behaviour You don't even think of a baby. All you're thinking of is the sexual activity – it eliminates the baby – emotionally, mentally, psychologically...Had I conceived, the next step for me would have been to eliminate the baby by an abortion. It is such a small step from mental elimination of the baby to its physical elimination. There's such a difference in contraceptive sexual activity and true marital intercourse.*" [1]

This lady's experience reflects exactly what Pope John Paul II wrote on the contraceptive mentality:

> "*It may be that many people use contraception with a view to excluding the subsequent temptation to abortion. But the negative values inherent in the "contraceptive mentality"...are such that they strengthen this temptation when an unwanted life is conceived.*" [2]

The statistical evidence indeed reveals that the majority of babies who are aborted were conceived during contraceptive intercourse. This is outlined in Appendix Three of this book. Abortion and contraception are closely connected, "*as fruits of the same tree*". [3]

> "*Abortion becomes the only decisive response to failed contraception.*" [4]

Contraception Stems the Graces of the Marriage Sacrament

Contraception stems the flow of grace of the marriage sacrament, grace essential for a lifelong, harmonious marriage. It directly contradicts one of the three essential components of marriage, that of openness to life.

This is because in marriage, the grace of the sacrament can only fully flow when the spouses place no obstacle in its path. [5] The sacrament bears the fullest spiritual fruits only in those who receive it with the correct dispositions. [6]

Couples speak of the loss of the sense of faith when they start using contraception. Gerard and Marie spoke about how contraception put a block between themselves and God. Tom and Mary related exactly the same thing.

---

[1] Personal Communication 2007

[2] EVn13

[3] cf EVn13

[4] EVn13

[5] cf CCn40 – 41

[6] cfCCCn1128,n1131

Using contraception, spouses no longer follow the Maker's instructions for their marriage. They no longer act in union with God's plan. Christ can no longer be fully welcomed into their lives. No wonder spouses can struggle with issues of love and fidelity when they use contraception. Marriage can be tough enough without depriving ourselves of sacramental, sanctifying graces.

Only when both couples turned back to God's plan for their marriage, and stopped using contraception, did they feel the block was removed.

Use of Contraception is Often Rooted in Fear

How often is contraception used because of fear - fear of having too many children, fear of not being able to cope, fear of making a bad marriage worse, of not having enough money? There's the fear of health risks, cramped lifestyles, or fear of bringing children into an evil world. There's the fear of being a second class citizen, 'shackled' and 'subjugated' as a mother at home all day.

One woman wrote of her sterilisation:

> "I felt I had solved all my problems – or so I thought. I had embraced everything the feminist movement promoted as being liberating and empowering for women. In reality, I had not been liberated; every day I felt more trapped in a bad marriage." [1]

"In reality, I had not been liberated; every day I felt more trapped"

a wife

Contraception doesn't solve problems. God doesn't want us to be crippled with fears about the number of children we have. Fear has no part in the Christian life. The scriptures tell us: *"Perfect love drives out all fear."* [2]

Contraception is the very opposite of perfect love. It is not the answer to fear. It brings its own pain. The way of Christ is the answer to all our fears. There is a better way to address such fears than contraception.

Contraceptive Intercourse is Not the Real Thing

Which would you prefer... a real £100 note or a fake one? If you had the choice, wouldn't you want the real thing? So it is with conjugal love.

Contraceptive intercourse is not the real thing. It falsifies the very meaning and purpose of marriage. Spouses settle for second best.

The two primary ends of marriage are union (bonding) and procreation (children). In contraception there is no more true union, no more openness to children and no more authentic love. It radically changes the nature of the marital act. No longer can the love and communion of husband and wife truly reflect that of the Blessed Trinity.

The real thing is worth striving for.

---

[1] cf Burke, T p17
[2] 1Jn 4:18

A Protestant Perspective

Sam Torode, co-author of the book *Open Embrace: A Protestant Couple Rethinks Contraception*, writes how contraception is destructive of love.

> *"I've read a good deal about the side-effects of contraception - especially hormonal varieties such as the Pill. As a husband, I can't imagine inflicting that upon my wife. (And this is not even to mention the greatest problem with the Pill - that it can act as an abortifacient.) The great struggle of being a Christian husband is working to love our wives as Christ loves the Church. We all fail at that, but contraception seems to me to be very destructive of love. Sex should be the very picture of self-giving love. At this time of greatest intimacy, contraception puts a barrier between husband and wife - a literal barrier, in the case of condoms and diaphragms."* [1]

Consider these words written from a Protestant perspective – *"contraception seems to me to be very destructive of love."*

TRUE Love Means Willingness for Parenthood

It is now easier to see why the marital act cannot be deprived of its procreative capacity without serious damage to true love:

> *"Love and parenthood must not...be separated one from each other. Willingness for parenthood is an indispensable condition for love."* [2]

Maintaining the attitude of 'willingness for parenthood' is what guarantees that total self-giving so essential to authentic marital union. Only then can there be a full and authentic union of persons.

> *"Willingness for parenthood is an indispensable condition for love"*
>
> Pope John Paul II

'Willingness' for parenthood doesn't necessarily mean a 'desire' for parenthood. Willingness for parenthood means that *should a conception occur*, the spouses are willing to accept it.

In God's plan, love and parenthood cannot be separated from each other. When they are, disharmony and division inevitably follow.

The Effects of Contraception – a Summary

To summarise the last two chapters, in using contraception:

×   Spouses view each other differently, and for many couples true communication can cease.

---

[1] http://www.neetje.net/INTERVIEWS.HTML, reproduced with permission
[2] LRp236

- × There is no true union. True love is replaced by the selfish pursuit of pleasure to the point of using the 'other'.

- × There is a sense of separation from each other. There can be a greater vulnerability to "look elsewhere" for fulfilment.

- × Deprived of its procreative dimension, the marital act is no longer an act of love.

- × There's a sense of separation from God and often a sense of loss of faith.

- × There is a disintegration of intimacy and closeness.

- × There is an increased risk of separation.

- × The graces of the marriage sacrament are blocked.

- × Spouses and their marriage are deprived of the blessings that children entail.

Chapter Ten

Just Why is Contraception Wrong?
The Rebellion Against God

"Through contraception, married couples ... claim a power which belongs solely to God."

Pope John Paul II

Claiming a power that belongs to God

What is wrong with contraception? Consider this statement from Pope John Paul II:

> *"When therefore, through contraception, married couples remove from the exercise of their conjugal sexuality its potential procreative power, THEY CLAIM A POWER WHICH BELONGS SOLELY TO GOD; the power to decide in a final analysis the coming into existence of a human person. They assume the qualification not of being co-operators in God's creative power but the ultimate depositaries of human life.*
>
> *In this perspective, contraception is to be judged so profoundly unlawful as never to be for any reason justified. To think or to say the contrary is equal to maintaining that in human life, situations may arise in which it is lawful not to recognise God as God."* [1]

Contracepting couples, even if they are unaware of it, are claiming for themselves a power that belongs to God. They take upon themselves the decision whether or not a new human being should come into existence! They have set themselves up as judges as to whether there will be new life or not.

By using contraception, they are rebelling against His command to be fruitful, to fill the earth and subdue it. They are refusing to be co-creators with God.

Consider again the Pope's statement;

---

[1] emphasis added: Pope John Paul II, Oct 10th 1983, cf Kippley p135-6

'contraception is to be judged so profoundly unlawful as never to be for any reason justified.'

Imagine that! Never to be for any reason justified! Why would the Pope, the Vicar of Christ, make such a bold statement?

The Question of Evil in the World

Contraception deeply alters the meaning and purpose of the marital act and its use has been termed *"intrinsically evil."* [1]

Evil in the world is an undeniable reality. Pope John Paul II observed:

> *"...life is always at the centre of a great struggle between good and evil, between light and darkness."* [2]

Like everyone else, married couples are caught up in this struggle of good and evil even in their sexual and intimate relations. [3] One characteristic of evil is that it causes human hearts to offer *"resistance to Christ."* [4] We are all continually faced with the challenge of being obedient to Christ or rebelling against Him in the choices we make. [5] So it is with regard to contraception.

Where the Problems First Began - The 'Fall' of Man

Satan, referred to in the *Catechism* as the Evil One, is the angel who opposes God. [6] He tempted the first man and woman, Adam and Eve, to disobey God – a primeval event which is termed the 'Fall' of man through original sin. [7] As a consequence, every human person has been affected by sin ever since. [8] Up to then, Adam and Eve had been in a state of perfect unity, love and communion. They also lived in perfect communion with God - perfect marital bliss! Indeed, their perfect union in marriage is held to be the model for every marriage today. [9]

With the Fall however, this perfect communion with God and each other was ruptured. With original sin came the inclination to evil, predisposing them to selfishness. Since the Fall, every marriage has been affected. [10]

Sin - a Revolt Against God

Contraceptive use has been termed a grave sin. [11]

---

[1] CCCn2370;cfTOBp398

[2] EVn104

[3] cf CCCn1607;cf TOB p376; CCCn409

[4] TOBp574

[5] cf TOBp191-197, CCCn396-421

[6] cf CCCn2851

[7] cf CCCn385-421;cf Genesis 3

[8] cf CCCn402-403

[9] cf CCn34; cf TOB p30

[10] cf CCCn1606-8; cf CCCn385-412

[11] cf CCn56

What IS sin?

> *"Sin...is disobedience, a revolt against God through the will to become 'like Gods', knowing and determining good and evil."* [1]

Sin is a revolt against God. It is disobedience towards God and a lack of trust in his goodness. [2] Since the Fall, every human being is engaged in the struggle between the inclination to sin or to exercise goodness and self-control. [3] Sin is attempting to become like God. That's the lie the serpent told Adam and Eve in the Garden of Eden. He told them if they ate the forbidden fruit, they would become like God and could decide what was good and what was evil. [4]

Satan tells the same lie today. Married couples are lied to; they are made to think they can claim a power that belongs to God, that they are "in control" (remember the term "birth-control"). They are led to believe that they can decide that evil is no longer evil. They are made to think that they are in control and that this is better than entrusting their lives to God.

What a massive lie!

Who's in Control?

Contraception, in effect, causes spouses to offer resistance to Christ in their marriage and its use is always (intrinsically) evil, irrespective of the circumstances. For spouses to use contraception reveals a lack of understanding of what marriage is about and its use is disobedience to God's will for marriage.

A married acquaintance of mine told me one day how *SHE* controlled when her children arrived. She said she had used the pill to turn on and off her child-bearing at will. However, what she didn't realise is that a child is not a right or a commodity to be switched on and off at will, but is a gift from God with whom spouses cooperate when the Giver of the gift decides to send such a gift. By using contraception, spouses are in effect saying 'we'll control when we have a child, not God'. They are thus attempting to become like God, which, as we have just seen, is the very definition of sin.

It is the couple's duty to discern and follow God's will and not for them to control when or how many children they will have. That is God's prerogative.

In the struggle for Victory

The ultimate victory of good over evil, death and darkness *is absolutely assured*, but we still have our part to play. [5] Pope John Paul II highlights we all are involved in

---

[1] CCCn1850
[2] cf CCCn397
[3] cf Gal 5:16–26
[4] cf Genesis 3:5
[5] cf EVn25

an "*enormous clash*" between the "*culture of death*" and the "*culture of life*" and every person has the "*inescapable responsibility of choosing to be unconditionally pro-life.*" [1]

St. Paul exhorts us not to allow any part of our bodies to turn into an unholy weapon fighting on the side of sin. Instead "*...you should make every part of your body into a weapon fighting for the side of God.*" [2]

Is the use of contraception in a Christian marriage not a form of spiritual mutiny? Do contracepting spouses not reduce their effectiveness in the fight? Contraception depletes Christ's army of countless soldiers. How many millions didn't even get the chance to fight, leaving the rest of us struggling with weakened ranks?

Contraception Opposes Man's Fundamental Vocation to Love

We see more clearly now how the use of contraception opposes man's vocation to love .

Love is the fundamental vocation of each one of us. [3] The very nature of love finds itself rooted in the nature of God, who IS love.

Using the contraceptive pill is not like taking an aspirin. It is not a case of merely taking a pill to bring about an intended therapeutic change in the body. Contraception is a product, the effect of which cuts at the very essence of what it is to be human, to be masculine, to be feminine, to be a person.

> *Contraception opposes real love in the life of everyone it touches.*

Contraception opposes the total self-giving demanded by real love and it opposes true spousal communion. It opposes man's vocation to love on the earth – to be gift to another. [4] It opposes real love in the life of everyone it touches.

There is Hope!

However, irrespective of the difficulties in any marriage, there is always a way to better harmony. There is abundant evidence to show that rejection of contraception greatly improves a troubled marriage.

A wife wrote:

> "*Despite my years of contraceptive use, and having lived away from our Catholic faith, which caused us much unhappiness and regret, my husband and I are now back in our faith with a fervour and determination to remain protected within the boundaries God has set up for us. We refuse now to get involved in anything against Catholic teaching.*

---

[1] cf EVn28
[2] Rom 6:13
[3] cf FCn11
[4] cf TOBp63

I rejoice in the fact that God is a loving, merciful, forgiving, understanding, caring, and bountiful God who loves me unconditionally and eternally without resentment or prejudice." [1]

A return to obedience of God's plan for love, life and procreation is the way to a stronger marriage, a more harmonious relationship and truly enriching, honest acts of loving marital union. [2]

Christ is there every day to take us back irrespective of our past. There is no situation too difficult. We are encouraged that:

> *"No difficulty can arise that justifies putting aside the law of God which forbids all acts intrinsically evil. There is no possible circumstance in which husband and wife cannot, strengthened by the grace of God, fulfil faithfully their duties and preserve in wedlock their chastity unspotted."* [3]

> "I rejoice in the fact that God is a loving, merciful, forgiving, understanding, caring, and bountiful God who loves me unconditionally and eternally."
> (MM)

Imagine that! There is *"no possible circumstance"* where spouses cannot - with God's grace - remain faithful to their spouses and their marriage vows.

The Church a Sign of Contradiction

The Church is not afraid of its message in the modern world. Pope Paul VI wrote a bold passage on how the Church sees itself as a messenger and not as an author of God's teaching on human sexuality and contraception in today's world:

> *"It can be foreseen that this teaching will perhaps not be easily received by all...To tell the truth, the Church is not surprised to be made, like her divine founder, a "sign of contradiction", yet she does not because of this cease to proclaim with humble firmness the entire moral law, both natural and evangelical. Of such laws the Church was not the author, nor consequently can she be their arbiter; she is only their depositary and their interpreter."* [4]

A key question to consider; Has the Catholic Church truly been divinely appointed by Christ to be *THE* authentic interpreter of the Creator's laws in matters of faith and morals? Does the evidence we are now examining concur with its claim that it speaks with *"the mind of Christ"*? [5]

---

[1] MM Personal communication Aug 2007

[2] cf HVn13-16;cfHVn21

[3] CCn61

[4] HVn18

[5] cfCCCn389

The Wisdom of the Church

Here are a few comments on the Church by my wife:

"The Church is not stupid or unrealistic. She is not a pushover. Over the years She has become more and more aware of the scientific developments of our time. She has witnessed the struggle of man and the flesh in daily life, the world over for centuries. And in all that time, She has promoted the good of man. She speaks as a mother who loves her children.

Whatever her children think of her, She loves them, teaches them, and just like I do with my own children, She lays out a way of living that is for their good. The children may not like it, but does that mean it should change?

When my two year old wants to go near the fire, I say "no, it's dangerous". He might shout, argue, or even try to defy my word. Should I change my mind to keep him happy? No, of course not.

If he wants to stick something in the electrical socket, should I let him because he "needs to explore the world around him"? Nonsense! It would mean death to him...He does not know that, nor would he care...he just wants to do it - whatever the consequences. I am his parent and I have a duty to protect him. I have more experience and more wisdom than he has and I have to draw the line.

So how much wisdom does the Church have? Two thousand years of parenting with six billion children on earth today! I'd listen to a parent with that much wisdom and experience, wouldn't you?"

Chapter Eleven

The Wider Social Picture
of Contraception

*Europe is contracepting
itself into oblivion*

Is Contraception a Private Decision
Between Two People?

Some argue that contraceptive use is a private decision between two people. 'What business is it of anyone else?' they say.

The use of contraception affects everyone directly or indirectly.
Not only does contraception directly affect the spouses in their love, communion, harmony and marital stability, it also deprives them of the blessings of offspring. It deprives children already born of the benefit of brothers and sisters. It deprives society of citizens. It deprives the ranks of God's army in the universal, cosmic fight against sin.

In Northen Ireland, a small country of 1.5 million people, 50,000 secondary school places remain unfilled compared to fifteen years ago. Many schools are closing down and amalgamating because of the lack of pupils. How many doctors, nurses, teachers, farmers, musicians, artists, priests, religious and workers of every conceivable trade and vocation has this country been deprived of because of contraception? The problem is worldwide. Could one of these 'lost children' have been destined to be the discoverer of the cure for AIDS or cancer?

I recently visited Italy for a family wedding. It is a country that is committing demographic suicide by not replacing itself. Statistically, every country needs an average of 2.1 children per couple to sustain and replace its population. Italy's birth rate is 1.18. I was struck by the fact there were no children playing in the streets. Germany's birth rate is 1.38. Holland's is 1.8, Finland's is 1.8 and Ireland's is 1.9. Europe is contracepting itself into oblivion.

Fr Paul Marx, a sociologist, has often asked the question of what will happen, sociologically speaking, if the followers of Islam, whose culture places a great emphasis on large families, outnumber the native inhabitants in those European countries which are suffering plunging rates through contraception?

One of the tenets of Islam is the conversion of the whole world to Islam. In a widely reported survey conducted by an independent market research company amongst the 40,000 Muslims in Ireland, 57% of young Muslims surveyed are reported to hold the view that Ireland should become an Islamic state, while 36% of those surveyed believed Ireland should be ruled by Sharia law.[1]

In Finland, it is reported that Europe's first Islamic political party has been formed with a manifesto that includes plans to introduce Sharia law into the country.[2] In September 2008, it was widely debated if the verdict of Sharia law courts in Britain can now be legally binding under UK law and enforced by county courts or the High Court.[3]

For Muslim folk to have lots of children as their faith encourages is no bad thing. Muslim people are fine defenders of family and life at a United Nations level in conjunction with the Catholic Church and developing countries. There is no problem if different peoples, races and faith choose to live peaceably side by side, respecting one another's differences and cultures.

> The real problem
> is that a
> contracepting
> western world is
> eliminating itself
> with its plunging
> birth rates
> leaving itself
> vulnerable

The immediate issue however is not with Islam or any perceived or potential challenge posed by Islam. The real problem is that a contracepting western world is eliminating itself with its plunging birth rates leaving itself vulnerable to any number of potential scenarios.

Then there is the pension crisis in Britain and Western Europe. Because of plummeting birth rates, there are now insufficient young people in the workforce to sustain the pension system. Experts are forecasting imminent drastic revisions of the system.[4]

Then there is the ideological element. How many contraceptive users realise they are pawns in a massive global contraceptive promotion geared to world population reduction? As well as the massive financial interests, in western countries the contraceptive marketing is pitched to appealingly entice users into believing they are 'freely' choosing to be responsible without informing them of a bigger picture.

In developing countries, relief aid from richer nations is tied to compulsory acceptance of mass contraceptive and sterilisation programmes to reduce populations of under-developed countries. This policy is motivated by the intent of protecting access to valuable raw materials and strategic resources for the richer nations in developing countries.[5]

Most users today don't realise that modern day contraceptive promotion still finds its roots in Margaret Sanger's eugenic, elitist, class discriminatory, racist

---

[1] cf *Irish Independent* Tuesday Dec 19th 2006; Landsdowne Market Research Survey

[2] cf *Irish Catholic*, 20 September 2007, p8

[3] cf wwwdailymailonline.co.uk 15 September 2008

[4] "Work Till You Drop! The Grim Message to Britain: Forget Retirement" *Daily Express* September 5th 2008 p1 & p5

[5] NSSM 200, Kissinger, Henry, National Security Study Memorandum 200, April 24, 1974: implications of worldwide population Growth for US Security and Overseas Interests, Initiating Memo.

and anti-religion ideology as described in Chapter Four. They are unwittingly caught up in clash between two diametrically opposed worldviews as further outlined in Appendix Five.

Two books that expose the blatant deception of the masterminds behind contraception promotion are 'Blessed are the Barren – The Social Policy of Planned Parenthood' by Marshall and Donovan and 'Grand Illusions' by George Grant. Both are cited in the reference list at the beginning of this book.

Whether the strategies are enticement or coercion, the outcome is the same; human beings are thwarted in their billions from ever even existing on the earth.

As already discussed, what about all the lives cut short by the abortifacient nature of the pill and other so-called contraceptives causing the death of children just after conception?[1] It is occurring all around us - in our bedrooms, in homes, streets, villages, towns, cities and countries. It may not be so obvious but it is none the less real.

There are six billion people on the earth, each made in the image of God. It is horrifying to think that by using contraception we are thwarting the kingdom of God of countless citizens who each were destined to a vocation on earth. What of the eternal destiny of each of these people who were to be? Spouses do not have the right to affect other lives as such by using contraception. They are not creators. They are co-creators with God.

Contraception is not just a private decision.

No wonder, then, that *Humanae Vitae* states that husband and wife, in the responsible exercise of parenthood:

> "*recognise fully their own duties towards God, towards themselves, towards the family and towards society, in a correct hierarchy of values.*" [2]

There is a wider picture to all our actions.

---

[1] see appendix 2
[2] HVn10

Who knows how many more children
should be in our classrooms?

Part Three

The Way to a Better Marriage

Chapter Twelve

Natural Family Planning (NFP)
A Step in the Right Direction

*"NFP wiped away the boredom that had entered
our marriage with the pill"*

Gerard and Marie

Many couples have transformed their marriages by turning away from contraception and choosing natural family planning.

*"It bonded my husband and me...
in a way that is so deep, so strong"*
a wife

We went to the Sacrament of Confession
and a thousand ton weight was
lifted off our shoulders. I felt free
and close to God again. There was no
barrier between me and God anymore
Tom, husband

"I fell in love... all over again!"
Gerard, husband

*"We couldn't have done it had we
not surrendered ourselves to God"*
Marie, wife

*"It challenged me to self-mastery
so that I can give freely, give myself"*
a husband

One Woman's Experience

Here is the experience of one lady who came to reject contraception in her life:

> *"Yes, I was alive and fertile in 1968. I was 19 and I knew the pill was a gift from God and Humanae Vitae was a real crock. The pill was going to eliminate teenage pregnancy, marital disharmony and the world population problem..."*

She recounts the relational difficulties she had in her marriage when she was contracepting. Then:

> *"Finally, my husband and I reached a turning point. At a very low point in our marriage, we met some great people who urged us to really give our lives to the Lord and be chaste in our marriage. That blew our minds. We thought it meant 'give up sex'. That's not what it means. It means respecting bodily union as a sacred act. It meant acting like a couple in love, a couple in awe, not a couple of cats in heat.*
>
> *For my husband and me, it meant NFP...and I won't kid you, it was a difficult discipline. NFP and a chaste attitude towards sex in marriage opened up a whole new world for us. It bonded my husband and me in a way that is so deep, so strong, that it's hard to describe. Sometimes its difficult, but that makes us even closer. We revere each other. And when we come together, we're like honeymooners.*
>
> *Sad to say, I was past 35 when I finally realized that the Church was right after all...The Church is right about contraception (it stinks), right about marriage (it's a sacrament) right about human happiness ‑ it flows – no, it floods when you embrace the will of God. It gave us depth. It opened our hearts to love."* [1]

This woman discovered a transformation in her marriage when she changed from contraception to natural family planning (NFP). Her comments illustrate what we have already alluded to: that happiness flows when you embrace the will of God, that the marital act which is open to life brings great strength to a marriage and a sense of deep fulfilment. It brings spouses closer together.

These comments could be repeated by many couples who have ditched contraception and embraced God's will for their marriage. If you are using contraception, you too can do the same.

Marital Acts Open to Life

In the following pages you will read the extraordinary effect on marriages that occurs when couples choose to leave EVERY marital act open to life.

You will read how couples rejected contraception and how they found natural family planning transformed their lives. You will read the stories of other couples who discovered the freedom that comes when they feel that they don't even need NFP.

---

[1] *National Catholic Reporter*, October 31st 1986

NFP is morally acceptable where circumstances are serious enough to merit its use. It brings great blessings to a marriage.

Let's examine what studies say about the use of NFP.

Less than 5% Divorce Rate Among NFP Users

"Dramatic low divorce with NFP"- states one study citing a 0.2% rate for NFP users.[1]

"... a 5% divorce rate among couples practicing NFP is really the outside maximum limit." [2]

Extravagant claims? Let's look at the evidence.

In the USA, contraceptive usage is reported to be used by approximately 73% of married women of child bearing age.[3] The divorce rate in USA is 40-50%. In contrast, the divorce rate is reported to range from 0.2% - 5% amongst users of modern versions of Natural Family Planning.[4]

A Clinical Science

What is 'natural family planning'? Is it not Catholic contraception? How does it transform marriages and how can it be morally acceptable when contraception isn't?

One crucial point must be made. Modern natural family planning is now a thoroughly researched science that has been highly refined. It can be used effectively to space births by any couple irrespective of religion, race or class.

Studies in China, India, South America, Korea, the USA, Europe and Australia prove its effectiveness even with users of high poverty and illiteracy levels. It has been officially endorsed as a means of birth regulation by the Chinese Government.[5]

Just because the Catholic Church allows NFP in certain circumstances, it does not make it merely a 'Catholic birth control' method.

99.7% Effective in Spacing Births

Effective child spacing can be achieved by NFP. By observing the natural biological signs of a woman's menstrual cycle, the modern methods

Modern natural family planning is now a thoroughly researched science that has been highly refined

---

[1] www.familyplanning.net
[2] Kippley, Art of NFP p245
[3] cf www.unstats.un.org
[4] see also De Stoop p63
[5] www.woomb.org

of natural family planning (NFP) show statistical effectiveness rates of up to 99.7% for avoiding pregnancy.[1]

This is as good and indeed more effective in postponing conception as contraception methods and has no medical side-effects or consequences. The method is highly effective even in women with irregular cycles. No drugs or invasive artificial devices are involved. These figures should reassure married couples who are concerned about having too many children.

How Does it Help Space Births?

The Billings, Creighton and Sympto-thermal methods of Natural Family Planning (NFP) are three modern, clinically proven methods of effective child spacing. They replace the out-dated, discredited and unreliable "rhythm" or "calendar" method.

They rely on monitoring the consistency and appearance of cervical mucus which varies on a daily basis throughout the menstrual cycle. In addition, the daily temperature fluctuations that occur with each cycle can be monitored if using the Sympto-thermal method. Observing these signs enables couples to identify the day when they are most likely to conceive during each menstrual cycle.

So effective is it in identifying a woman's peak day of fertility each month, that NFP is also used effectively to achieve pregnancy by couples struggling with infertility.

It is necessary to consult a trained practitioner to avail of NFP properly. See websites cited in Appendix Seven.

NFP Greatly Promotes Marital Harmony

In practicing natural family planning, spouses work closely together monitoring the signs of fertility throughout the monthly cycle. Several studies indicate that the practice of NFP increases marital stability and improves marital harmony.[2]

In these studies the majority of NFP users reported:

- × greater intimacy
- × improved communication
- × shared responsibility
- × greater mutual respect
- × improved appreciation of sexuality

---

[1] Hilgers, T.W., Stanford, J.B., Creighton Model NaproEducation Technology for avoiding pregnancy. Use effectiveness. *Journal of Reproductive Medicine* 43:6, 495-502, June 1998; R. E. J. Ryder, "Natural family planning': Effective Birth Control Supported by the Catholic Church,' *British Medical Journal*, Sept. 18,1993. 307:723-726; cfWilson; cf www.naomi.ie and www.wooomb.org

[2] cfVandeVusse, cf Shivanandan;cf Wilson

- × improved knowledge of body
- × enriched spirituality
- × greater self-control
- × enhanced relationships
- × decreased selfishness
- × better health
- × deeper love

Why Does NFP Bring These Remarkable Benefits to a Marriage?

NFP allows all marital acts to remain 'open to life'. As a result the couple reaps a wealth of benefits for themselves and their marriage.

The mutually shared responsibility required by couples for successful NFP often opens up a dimension of communication that did not exist before.

There is another important factor why NFP brings so many benefits and that is, surprisingly, abstinence. Let's look at this more closely.

Chapter Thirteen

The Transforming Power
of Abstinence

*"It was precisely the abstinence entailed
each month in NFP that fuelled and renewed
my great desire and love for my wife."*

Gerard, Husband

Gerard and Marie's Story Continued

GERARD: "When natural family planning was explained to me, I had an instant recognition of what was happening in my wife's body. I didn't understand my own fertility, let alone hers. It was precisely the abstinence entailed each month in NFP that fuelled and renewed my great desire and love for my wife. It was like a flashback to how I'd felt when we were engaged - I so wanted to make love to her but it wasn't the right time. NFP wiped away the boredom that had entered our marriage with the pill. When we started to chart her fertility, we had to abstain for 28 days. During those days I had a huge shift of perspective; when I couldn't have it - then I really wanted it! I fell in love with Marie all over again."

The Abstinence Factor *Enhances* Intimacy

Gerard makes a pivotal statement about NFP:

> *"It was precisely the abstinence entailed each month in NFP that fuelled and renewed my great desire and love for my wife."*

This type of comment is repeated many times by husbands and wives but especially by husbands; the period of abstinence each month triggered greater desire and love for their wives.

Couples reported that, despite the challenges entailed, it was precisely the abstinence and self-restraint each month that enhanced the anticipation and intimacy of conjugal relations.[1] The wife becomes more desirable with abstinence and the husband becomes more respected in his wife's eyes when she sees him exercising self-restraint for love of her.

---

[1] cf VandeVusse

The Transformation

Gerard and Marie continue...

MARIE: "I felt more loved and cherished. I understand how a woman using contraception can feel used. In the abstinence periods, we had to find other ways of saying 'I love you'. It became a case of 'you are more important' rather than 'sex is more important'. Even with the pill, where there was no physical barrier, it still felt like there was a barrier."

> "It became a case of 'you are more important' rather than 'sex is more important' "
>
> Marie

GERARD: "We only noticed the barrier was there once it was gone. Now I am making love to a beautiful woman and I am totally free. Now we are vulnerable to each other and to God. With my body, I am saying: "how much I appreciate you". It puts sexuality on a totally different plane. We regard our children now as living manifestations of our love!"

MARIE: "It was the making of our marriage. We would have been two elderly people sitting in separate rooms out of touch with each other."

GERARD: "We took a chance on Pope Paul VI. It put life back into our marriage. Where we are today is a direct result of Humanae Vitae. I discovered recently the Popes are buried underneath St. Peters Cathedral in tombs. I want to go and apologise to Paul VI for railing against him - to ask forgiveness for being so vehement against him."

MARIE: "The road of NFP has its challenges. At times it's not easy. It's only by the grace of God that it can be done. The couple must be graced for their situation – It cannot be imposed upon them. We couldn't have done it if we hadn't surrendered ourselves to God."

Gerard and Marie's story vividly illustrates the return of the sparkle to their love once they gave up contraception and began practicing NFP. They mentioned the freedom they subsequently enjoyed and their words reflect what Pope John Paul II wrote whilst a Cardinal in the 1960's about 'person' first: where there is no contraception 'you' are more important than the 'sex'.

Like other couples who have journeyed on a similar road, they reported a deepening sense of being in tune with God and surrendering themselves in trust to Him.

Abstinence Means Better Dialogue

Gerard and Marie's experience echoes what studies have shown: that the abstinence and dialogue required with natural family planning open channels of communication and intimacy that are not present with contraception.

For a couple wishing to postpone a conception, NFP allows 18-21 days in each cycle when a couple can engage in the marital act and requires 7 -10 days of abstinence. The abstinence periods help couples cultivate other chaste forms of intimacy and expressions of love that deepen the bonds of their marriage.

Entirely New Attitude

Couples switching from contraceptive use to NFP report an entirely new attitude to their spouses and themselves. Mere gratification no longer becomes the principal motivation for expression of marital love and acts.

Somehow, maintaining that openness for parenthood keeps that spark in a couples' marital love. It does something for the way they view each other. Earlier, one lady cited put it this way:

> "I never truly felt loved by him until I saw his willingness to sacrifice and honour the cycles of my body."

Men appear to struggle the most with abstinence but their testimonies reveal it is worth the effort. As one man observed:

> "In sexual abstinence we find the challenge to <u>truly</u> love one another and care for each other in ways and on levels which without abstinence we would never be challenged to attain." [1]

Somehow, maintaining that 'openness for parenthood' … keeps that 'spark' in a couples' marital love.

Another husband comments:

> "I see NFP as an important contributor to my ongoing growth as a male and to marital happiness. It challenged me to self-mastery so that I can freely give my "self". [2]

Another husband likened abstinence to any other burden in married life "*which in the end are blessings.*" He writes:

> "*taking up this cross can strengthen our knowledge of ourselves and can increase the love and bonding between a husband and wife as we struggle on the paths of salvation.*" [3]

---

[1] Shivanandan p265
[2] Shivanandan p264
[3] Shivanandan p265

These words illustrate what Pope John Paul II wrote about the role of self-mastery in the development of the human person.[1] Self-sacrifice and self-mastery are positive goods.

One lady who had formerly used barrier methods now described their conjugal life as "fantastic". She said:

> *"Giving our whole selves intensified the sensations of pleasure and the feeling of unity in this expression of our love."*

She added that her husband:

> *"... respects me as a person in my own right. He accepts my fertility as part of me."*[2]

Her comment reflects what many wives discover when a couple take the NFP route – an entirely different attitude of the husbands towards their wives. She feels respected as a *PERSON*.

Her words *"He accepts my fertility as part of me"* mirrors what the Church teaches when it says that fertility is an integral part of the human person, not to be separated like a commodity from the other aspects of a person.

Tom and Mary's Dramatic Turnaround

As we read earlier, Tom and Mary's marriage reached rock bottom during contraceptive use.

A few days after Mary cried out in desperation to God for help, a neighbouring married couple and their children called in for a few minutes with a Christmas card and chocolates.

MARY: "The married couple invited us up to their home the following week for coffee. Their visit made us believe somebody cared."

TOM: "The day I visited their home, I was very keen to have a vasectomy. I was due to have it a few days later and was totally comfortable about the idea. However, at that house something happened. God touched me. I saw that what I was about to do (the imminent vasectomy) was offending God. It wasn't anything they said - it was just being there.

I walked out of that house a changed man. After that, there was no more contraception for myself or my wife. We went to the sacrament of confession and a thousand ton weight was lifted off our shoulders. I felt free and close to God again. There was no barrier between me and God anymore."

MARY: "We started using NFP again."

---

[1] TOBp368
[2] Shivanandan p266

TOM: "We gave God our marriage and we gave Him the following Lent by abstaining from sexual relations. We wanted to make up for what we'd done. We consecrated our lives to Our Lady and it really changed us. Our Lady came in and rearranged our lives."

MARY: "We started to talk about more children after Easter. We are so privileged because of the grace we've received. What would have happened if Tom had the vasectomy? We wouldn't be sitting here now looking forward to another baby – to lots more!"

TOM: "If I'd had that vasectomy we probably would have split up – all the grace would have gone out of our lives. If a couple is honest, it's usually the man who pursues the wrong practices. He is compromising her body, her purity. It is degrading to use a woman to fulfil your desires. Now I shudder about what I thought of her."

MARY: "Using contraception corrupts your mind, your thoughts and behaviour. Everything gets turned upside down and if your prayer life slips as well, your whole concept of marriage slips too. It's easy to see how people with no faith use contraception."

TOM: "Contraception means having sex. Children don't come into it. NFP however brings up discussion about having children. Then you begin to think 'why are we using it?' I now believe NFP should only be used for grave circumstances. God has made us see that he provides for anything he creates. We're glad we didn't space any of our children. We couldn't think of not having any of them. The closer you get to God the more open to life you become. All the fears start to leave you. We wouldn't want anyone to go through the same hell that we went through when we used contraception."

> "We wouldn't want anyone to go through the same hell that we went through when we used contraception."
>
> Tom and Mary

MARY: "We are SO happy about this pregnancy (the sixth). It's like a first pregnancy all over again, like starting from the beginning again in our relationship."

TOM: "We'd like many more children." [1]

Availing of God's Grace

This is a marvellous story of how God touched a young couple with the grace of conversion. Tom and Mary are still working through a healing process. Contraception causes a great deal of damage and takes a long time to heal.

---

[1] Tom and Mary, N Ireland, Personal Communication, 22 Nov 2006

Their experience illustrates the transformation that adopting NFP can have in a couple's marriage once they leave every marital act open to life and practice periodic abstinence. It is a powerful example of how the couple's attitude changed when they turned to God, gave Him their lives, and trusted in Him. They also testify to the presence of Mary, the Mother of Jesus, in their lives.

The Benefits of Abstinence

The benefits experienced by married couples are reflected in *Humanae Vitae's* 1967 synopsis which is strikingly relevant today:

> "Yet this discipline [periodic abstinence] which is proper to the purity of married couples, far from harming conjugal love, rather confers on it a higher human value. It demands continual effort yet, thanks to its beneficent influence, husband and wife fully develop their personalities, being enriched with spiritual values. Such discipline bestows upon family life fruits of serenity and peace, and facilitates the solution of other problems; it favors attention for one's partner, helps both parties to drive out selfishness, the enemy of true love; and deepens their sense of responsibility. By its means, parents acquire the capacity of having a deeper and more efficacious influence in the education of their offspring; little children and youths grow up with a just appraisal of human values, and in the serene and harmonious development of their spiritual and sensitive faculties".[1]

As with many other couples who have embraced the path of openness to life instead of contraception, Tom and Mary's attitude and openness about having children changed. Recognising and discussing fertility signs fosters an affirmation of the possibility of children with each marital act rather than eliminating the possibility.

An awareness is cultivated that this marriage, and the possible procreative consequences springing forth from it, is lifelong. This sense of lifelong commitment grows and becomes stronger.

God's grace is available to everyone.[2] As you read this, if you are in a contraceptive marriage, perhaps you feel God is calling YOU TOO, with your spouse, to turn back to him and his merciful love.

Four Steps Contracepting Couples
Need to Address

Psychotherapist and Deacon Dr. Bob McDonald prescribes a four step process for a couple who have realised that contraception is hurting their marriage and no longer wish to embrace it.

He said each spouse must say to themselves:

---

[1] HVn21
[2] TOBp366-7

1) I accept I have been engineering my own marital breakdown.

2) I have to repent of my self-centredness and my poverty of love.

3) I must surrender my entire self and especially my fertility first to God and then to my spouse.

4) I must proceed from now on with a total, complete trust in God and His plan for my spouse and myself.[1]

Dr. MacDonald's advice reflects Monsignor Cormac Burke's experience of dealing with couples struggling from marriage breakup:

> "Contraceptive couples who stop to reflect realize that their marriage is troubled by some deep malaise...Only a resolute effort to break with contraceptive practices can heal the sickness affecting their married life." [2]

> *"Only a resolute effort to break with contraceptive practices can heal the sickness affecting their married life"*
>
> Cormac Burke

Enduring Sexual Attraction

Raising the matter of enduring sexual attraction, author Christine de Stoop relates:

> "There aren't many women over forty whose husbands still chase them around the kitchen except the people who practice NFP." [3]

She speaks about the beauty of women:

> "Couples who do nothing to interfere with their fertility find that they will enjoy an enduring sexual attraction. Fluctuating cyclic hormones are quelled by Ocs (oral contraceptives), yet these (cyclic natural hormones) are known to make a woman feel and look attractive. Her interest in her looks and grooming is heightened and her energy level is raised. Even the way she moves, her natural smell and the way she uses her eyes and unconsciously fills her spouse's space will turn his head for decades. This is nature's plan to sustain a magnetism that contributes to the beauty of a woman." [4]

An intimate marital life 'open to life' flows with benefits and blessings.

---

[1] McDonald
[2] Burke, Cp38
[3] cf de Stoop p54
[4] ibid

The SPICE in Marriage

We have already seen that, in couples who undertake the challenge of NFP, wives find their husband's attitude towards them changed. The abstinence fosters an ethos of love which is lived out in a thousand ways between spouses each day. Leading NFP researcher Dr. Thomas Hilgers identified this ethos of love as a key root of marital satisfaction when he wrote:

> *"Genital intercourse is meant to be an optional expression of mental intercourse...Indeed the human brain is the centre and basis of all sexual intimacy between a man and a woman."* [1]

A husband demonstrates this 'mental sexual intimacy' in countless little ways; changing the nappies, rising to a crying child in the middle of the night, the squeeze of a hand in a crowded street, a hug, a visit to the coffee shop, the gift of a simple chocolate bar when he arrives home from work in the evening... all these little expressions of self-sacrifice and thinking of the other person are part of the wholeness of love. Christine de Stoop puts it beautifully:

> *"A man in love is always satisfied when the fruit of his personal sacrifice is manifested in the sexual receptivity of a woman who is deeply moved by his selfless love."* [2]

The self -mastery required by NFP also plays its part. Self-giving, self-sacrifice and loving the other before self will bring true marital satisfaction. It is not an easy road for anyone, but the best road to go nonetheless.

---

[1] cf de stoop p45
[2] de Stoop p47

Chapter Fourteen

Seven Key Principles of
Responsible Parenthood

"Reflecting upon this matter before God… parents will remind themselves that it is certainly less serious to deny their children certain comforts or material advantages than to deprive them of the presence of brothers or sisters, who could help them grow in humanity, and to realise the beauty of life at all its stages and in all its variety."

Pope John Paul II

All Babies and No Fun?

In the words of one woman, does the Catholic Church's teaching on procreation mean *"babies, babies, babies"* and *"no fun"*? What exactly does the Catholic Church say about the marital act and the spacing of births? How many children should you have?

There are guiding principles for married couples about the responsible spacing of children – what the Church terms 'responsible parenthood'. These principles can be applied to just about any situation, even the most difficult. It is recognized that physical, economic, psychological, medical, social and other conditions can affect decisions about responsible spacing of births.[1]

Seven key principles are summarised below.

1) SPOUSES MAY GENEROUSLY DECIDE TO RAISE A LARGE FAMILY OR, IN GRAVE CIRCUMSTANCES, POSTPONE A NEW BIRTH.[2]

For "grave" motives or "just" reasons , not "trivial" or "selfish" ones, spouses can legitimately postpone a new birth by moral means if circumstances are serious enough. This postponement may be for an indefinite time.[3] Each

---

[1] cf HVn10;n16, Allocution to Italian Union of Midwives 1951
[2] cf HVn10
[3] cf CCCn2368, cf HVn10, Kippley, Art of NFP p226;p229;p236, cf Smith, A Reader pp454-466, cf Barreiro, Ignacio, "The Rightful Use of Natural Birth Regulation", *HLI Reports*, V. 19, n.1, January 2001, pp5,9 and 14

couple has a responsibility to prayerfully ascertain whether such a serious reason is present in their lives.

2) EVERY COUPLE IS TO DISCERN GOD'S WILL AT EACH STAGE FOR THEIR FAMILY SIZE.

Every husband and wife have an *'obligatory discernment of the indications of God's will concerning their family'.*[1] It is a matter of taking it day by day, month by month, child by child, act by act, prayerfully assessing personal and wider circumstances to discern what God's plans might be.[2]

3) THE CHURCH WILL NOT TELL INDIVIDUAL COUPLES HOW MANY CHILDREN THEY SHOULD HAVE.

The Church will not instruct a couple: "you should have 2, 3, 4 or 5 children etc". Instead it teaches: *"It is the married couple themselves who must in the last analysis arrive at these judgements before God."* [3] Prudence and generosity are two key concepts to be kept in mind in this decision-making arena. [4]

4) RESPONSIBLE PARENTHOOD IS NOT EXCLUSIVELY ABOUT LIMITING FAMILY SIZE.

As well as limiting family size, responsible parenthood can also mean the willingness to accept a larger family".[5] The Church makes special mention of those who: *"with a gallant heart, and with wise and common deliberation, undertake to bring up suitably even a relatively large family."* [6]

5) RESPONSIBLE   PARENTHOOD   REQUIRES   TRUST   IN   DIVINE PROVIDENCE.

Procreation requires trust in *'Divine Providence'.* In doing so, spouses glorify God and acquit themselves of the duties of their state.[7] God will not send a child to any couple that He cannot provide for. Of course, parents must balance the duty to procreate with the welfare of their present and future children.

6) SPOUSES MUST RESPECT THE DIVINE LAW AT ALL TIMES [8]

In seeking either to postpone or establish a conception, union and procreation must never be separated. Every marital act must remain open to

---

[1] Pope John Paul II, cf Kippley, SMC p74
[2] Pope John Paul II, cf Kippley SMC p123 , cf Kippley , Art of NFP p239
[3] Vademecum, reference 32, qtg GSn50
[4] cf GSn50;cf TOBp394
[5] TOBp402
[6] GSn50
[7] cf GSn50
[8] cf HVnl0

life. Artificial contraception can never be justified under any circumstances.[1]
Responsible parenthood requires the 'necessary dominion' of will and reason over instinct or passion.[2]

7)   PERIODIC ABSTINENCE CAN BE USED WHERE THERE ARE SERIOUS MOTIVES TO SPACE BIRTHS

In this scenario, natural family planning (NFP) can be legitimately used to space births.[3]

What Does Being Generous Really Mean?

Some couples simply do not have the health, ability or circumstances to opt for a larger family. Even having one or two children for some is indeed being generous.

The circumstances of every couple are unique and only they are in a position to know all the details. For couples who have no serious impediments however, being generous may mean having a large family. It may mean being willing to accept if necessary a more modest house, a less expensive car, fewer lavish holidays, not being able to do 'your own thing' or living as a married single.

Couples who freely choose a larger family, if their circumstances allow and should God grant them this blessing, are, in a unique way, visionaries. They can see beyond the visible. They are like those who sell everything to buy the pearl of great price. They are willing to relinquish short term, temporal comforts for a treasure of infinite and eternal value – giving life to another child. The blessings to them are beyond price – beyond this world. Too many are settling for too little for this short transient time on earth.

The responsibility of every married couple is to discover the will of God for their personal lives and marriage. Each should cultivate that spirit of obedience and docility to God's will as the sure route to fulfilment and peace.

My wife Therese has this to say:

> *"Fidelity to God's plan does not mean absence of struggle. Fidelity to God's plan does not mean no 'fun' anymore, nor does it mean 'babies, babies, babies'. It does mean moving and operating under the blessing of Almighty God. It does mean a more meaningful life – both with God and spouse. It does mean a higher chance of eternal happiness. Presented with all of that versus doing it on your own, which would you rather have? I'll take all the graces I can get, thanks! Believe me, I need them!"*

---

[1] Pope John Paul II cf Kippley, Art of NFP p135-6
[2] cf HVn10
[3] cf HVn16

Chapter Fifteen

Why Does Harmony Flow in a
Marriage Open to Life?

"We have to, and this is the most difficult part of marriage and family life – listen to HIM – the one who knows us best, the one who knows best outright… Jesus Christ must be centre of the marriage or it will not work."

Therese McCrystal

Allowing God to Dwell at the Centre

Fifteen years ago two friends of mine, John and Liz, were using the pill in their marriage, and felt troubled by it. One evening they invited me around to their home to talk with them. As I talked about the various aspects of contraception, they became convinced to stop using the pill. The next morning they went to the Sacrament of Confession and started NFP. Some months later they conceived and now are the proud parents of a teenage boy.

As one young man put it:

> *"NFP is putting ourselves in God's hands, totally allowing Him to work spiritually inside our marriage."* [1]

It is God's will that every marital act be open to the transmission of life. When spouses leave every act open to life, that is, not using contraception, they act according to how marriage was designed. [2] At the time of each act, the spouses bring their circumstances to God and proceed or abstain according to His will and their circumstances. Christ is allowed to dwell at the centre of the marriage.

However, it isn't just practicing NFP that allows God into the heart of your marriage. More accurately, it is the *openness to life* which allows the REAL flow of blessings.

---

[1] Shivanandan p267
[2] cf HVn13

Why does Harmony Flow in a Marriage Always Open to Life?

In a marriage open to life - where Christ truly reigns - true unity is maintained. The love of husband and wife expressed as total self-giving is preserved. Each gives their whole self, and each receives the whole of the other person as a gift in their marital acts. The procreative power of each is respected and accepted. Their mutual openness to parenthood predisposes them to willingness for shared sacrifice and life-long commitment to rear a child should he or she be conceived. God is free to act if He so wishes to bless this couple with another child. They can discern God's will regarding their family size. Their union flows towards greater fulfilment should a conception occur. Fidelity to each other is naturally enhanced.

In such a marriage, whether NFP is used or not, the spouses entrust themselves to the providence and design of the Creator. They have 'let go' and 'let God'. They grow more attuned to God together and in a greater trust in His will. He is allowed to dwell at the centre.

My wife believes that couples who grow together in trust in God:

> *"...will experience greater trust in each other. More trust means less fear. Less fear means more love. More love means a greater experience of life is lived, with the desire to share it. Love lives 'outwardly'. 'Self lives inwardly."*

The marital acts of the spouses open to life bring unparalleled sexual fulfilment and harmony. In those moments, their marriage resonates with the deepest purposes it was created for.

The discipline of abstinence and self-mastery flows into other areas of their lives. The graces of their sacrament remain unblocked and can flow richly, empowering them for the demands and challenges of their vocation. Spouses grow in the respect of each other and their bodies. Communication is honest and they enjoy an enduring attraction to one another.

"Love lives outwardly, Self lives inwardly"

THE Core Tenet of This Book

God is looking for married couples to be generous with life and generous with love, just as He is Himself. The truth is that God wishes every marital act to be open to life. There are no exceptions. That's the core tenet of this book. This does not mean that every marital act will result in a conception, or that this should be the intention. A conception obviously cannot occur during a woman's infertile time of the month, or in infertility or after the menopause. It means that any act may not be deliberately closed to life by contraceptive use.

God wishes couples to experience the freedom and joy that comes with trusting in Him according to the principles of responsible parenthood. He loves us deeply. He wishes us to live according to His laws of love, in freedom and spontaneity, without fear.

At the start of this book I said I believe God is looking for married couples who are willing to say 'yes' to children, 'yes' to love, 'yes' to life. I believe God is excited about marriage and is longing to bless you with your chosen spouse. He is longing for you to know real love and harmony with your spouse.

Call to True Conversion in Jesus Christ

The call of the Church, in its teaching on human sexuality and contraception, is nothing less than a call to true conversion in Jesus Christ.

It is a call to obey the perfect will of God in His plan for human love and sexuality. It is a call to be open to life, to love and to holiness.

It is a call, which, when followed humbly, perseveringly and truthfully, points the way to true marital harmony and peace.

Chapter Sixteen

NFP Can Be Abused

"We knew in our hearts that God wanted us personally not to use NFP and instead we decided to do our own thing."

John and Annette

A Great Blessing

It is a great blessing and a great relief to know that NFP is available as a safe, effective means to postpone another birth should circumstances require it. For a number of years I advocated NFP as the automatic and moral alternative to contraception. I was wrong however to advocate it without properly qualifying myself.

NFP is to be used only in serious or grave circumstances, for just reasons.[1] In such circumstances, it is morally acceptable for a couple to postpone conception for an indefinite period, even, if necessary, for the duration of their lives. For some couples however, using NFP is not necessary. Spouses need to be careful not to use NFP for the wrong motives.

John Kippley, author, theologian and father, puts it like this:

> *"For most of us, the question will not be "Are we obliged to avoid pregnancy?" For most of us, the recurring question will be "Are we justified in avoiding pregnancy right now?"* [2]

No Peace Whilst Practicing NFP

Here's the story of John and Annette who realised they were using NFP for the wrong reasons.

> *"After the birth of our fourth child, I began to fear getting pregnant again. Everyone told me I shouldn't get pregnant again, that I couldn't cope, and I began to wonder if they were right. I was trying to do things 'God's way' but other voices were calling me a different way.*
>
> *John and I decided to practice NFP. We knew that at least we were 'open to life' and not blocking God. The only problem was that we knew in our hearts that God*

---

[1] cfHVn16
[2] Kippley, Art of NFP p236

wanted us personally not to use NFP. Instead we decided to do our own thing. WE
took control into our own hands, instead of following His plan for our lives.
We had no peace at all practicing NFP. I could easily see how it could be used like
another contraceptive. We weren't allowing God's plan for us to unfold, and this
caused difficulties in our marriage.
We knew we weren't being completely open to each other and to life as God wished
at that time.

Eventually John and I decided God knew better and we would put our trust in
Him again. We abandoned NFP and allowed ourselves to be completely open to
God's plan: life. Then, when our fourth child Aaron was thirteen month old, I
became pregnant again...[1]

Natural Family Planning Can Be Misused

It is possible for couples to misuse NFP and come to view it as merely another type
of contraception. The world's media took note when Pope John Paul II pointed out
that NFP can be abused:

> *"The use of the "infertile periods" for conjugal union can be an abuse if the couple,*
> *for unworthy reasons, seeks in this way to avoid having children, thus lowering the*
> *number of births in their family below the morally correct level... One comes to the*
> *point of speaking of it {the natural method} as if it were only a different form of*
> *contraception."* [2]

So NFP may be misused for "unworthy reasons". To use NFP in this way can *"... be*
a sin against the very meaning of conjugal life." [3]

In such instances, abuse of NFP might even be robbing your marriage, and
the kingdom of God, of one of its most splendid, supreme gifts - a child.

A Huge Step Towards Improvement

Let's be clear on something. A couple who reject contraception and adopt instead
the principles of natural family planning have taken a *massive step* forward in
improving their lives and their marriages. They have taken a huge step in the right
direction.

Yes, it is true that the use of NFP to postpone pregnancy is more natural in
that it means the avoidance of artificial chemicals in the woman's body. Yes, it is
natural in that the use of NFP harnesses the natural fertility cycle of the wife to
avoid pregnancy. It is true that its use can help a woman more greatly appreciate
and understand her fertility. Yes, it is true that the use of NFP means that each
marital act is open to life - a morally crucial factor.

---

[1] *John and Annette, Belfast, 20 February 2006*
[2] Pope John Paul II, General Audience, 5th September 1984
[3] Allocution to Midwives 1951

However, in the absence of serious circumstances, many couples have discovered there is an even wider perspective than mere long-term use of NFP to space children.

Not Using NFP At All

After beginning NFP, many couples come to pleasantly realise that there are no serious reasons to continue using it. They find they have grown in trust in God's care and love for them. They find it easier to entrust their fertility to Him and relinquish their own 'control'.

A marriage open to life is truly an adventure. Imagine a scenario where husband and wife exercise the joy of their marital intercourse as freely as they wish with no concern or fear as to whether a child may result. Each is freely giving of self and freely receiving of the other. This is the sort of freedom and spontaneity every couple has the right to enjoy and exercise if they have no good reason not to have another child.

We are all infinitely better off with a marriage open to life, with Christ acting fully in our lives, with the number of children God wants and less savings, than only one or two children and thousands of pounds in the bank.

It is really amazing how God can provide for our needs in extraordinary ways. If we are following His will for our lives, we can trust Him to provide for us. Countless couples will attest to His provision, Therese and I included. Careful discernment and listening to God's voice in our lives is a key part of following His *unique* call for every couple.

A marriage open to life is truly an adventure.

Chapter Seventeen

The Difference Between Contraception and NFP

"When they are abstaining, couples using NFP can be compared to those who remain silent when it is better not to speak"

Dr. Janet Smith

What's the Difference Between Contraception and Natural Family Planning?

There is some controversy over how NFP can be different from the use of artificial contraception. Why is one morally acceptable but not the other? Aren't both used to prevent conception? Does their use not denote a lack of openness to new life?

The essential difference is that in NFP, a married couple make *"legitimate use of a natural disposition"*.[1] That is, they are harnessing the naturally occurring cycles of the female physiology. Such harnessing of the rhythms of fertility within the wife's monthly menstrual cycle are morally legitimate because it allows husband and wife to *"...respect the biological laws inscribed in their person"*.[2] Nothing is inserted to thwart the natural processes of their bodies. Their acts are still open to life. The procreative dimension is not removed. God is allowed to be God.

In contraception however, the couple *"offend the nature of the act"*[3] and *"impede the development of natural processes."*[4] There is a deliberate impeding or hindering of the natural act and thus the natural consequences. Contraception falsifies an act that denotes total self-giving.

Karol Wojtyla, later to become Pope John Paul II, noted that couples practising NFP however:

> *"...are merely adapting themselves to the laws of nature, to the order which reigns in nature... Nature makes procreation possible in the fertile period, and impossible in the infertile period. But deliberate prevention of procreation by human beings, acting contrary to the order and laws of nature is quite a different matter."*[5]

---

[1] cfHVn16
[2] Evn97
[3] Allocution to Midwives 1951
[4] cfHVn16
[5] LR p235

Couples may not expressly desire a child with every conjugal act they undertake, but the willingness to accept a child should a conception occur is a requirement that properly 'justifies' the act in a moral sense. In NFP, the act still remains 'open' to life.

NFP – 'Silence' Rather Than 'Lies'

Dr. Janet Smith uses a helpful analogy to compare the use of contraception with NFP – an analogy that my own wife found illuminating. She wrote:

> *"Clarification of the difference between contraception and natural family planning can also be made using the description of sexual intercourse as a kind of language through which the truth must be spoken...*
>
> *Pope John Paul II calls contracepted sexual intercourse a lie since it does not tell the truth, the truth of total self-giving that is proper to spousal intercourse.*
>
> *When they are abstaining, couples using NFP can be compared to those who remain silent when it is better not to speak. They think it is better not to speak the full language of love since this language may have results, that is, the conception of a child, that they think it is not right to invite at a given time.*
>
> *They are not falsifying an act that means total self-giving; they are refraining from such an act. And although it is clear that spouses having sexual intercourse during the infertile period are not giving quite as fully of themselves as they are during the fertile periods, they are not falsifying the act itself.*
>
> *They tell the truth that is to be told at a given time, they have given all there is to give at the time."* [1]

In a nutshell, couples using NFP are not falsifying the marital act, they are abstaining from the act. Couples using NFP are not 'telling a lie', they are 'remaining silent'.

There are many testimonies available about the dramatic improvement in the lives of couples who gave up contraception for a marriage that is ever *'open to life'*. [2]

For further information on NFP see Appendix 7.

---

[1] Smith, Janet E., *Humanae Vitae – A Generation Later*, Catholic University of America Press, Washington, 1991. Used with permission : The Catholic University of America Press, Washington DC p124

[2] cf www.omsoul.com The hurtful consequences of artificial contraception and sterilisation.
    Three interesting testimonies on these matters can be found on an audio cassette from: Human Life International (Ireland), 6 Belvedere Place, Dublin 1.

When they are abstaining, couples using NFP
can be compared to those who remain silent
when it is better not to speak.

Chapter Eighteen

Towards a Perfect Marriage

"Over the last 10 years our marriage has improved so dramatically. I don't think we even knew what love was."

former contraceptive user

The Way to Happiness - Embracing God's Will

"Happiness flows – no, it floods when you embrace the will of God" as quoted earlier from a former contraceptive user.

Christ, the Creator and Author of life and marriage Himself said:

"Rather, how happy are those who hear the word of God and obey it!"[1]

God speaks to us in many different ways. I have shared in this book some of the ways He has done that in my life. It is vital we learn to listen to His voice, His whisper, every day. I am teaching our children about seven ways God can speak to you:

1) Directly in your heart

2) Through the scriptures

3) Through those in authority in your life

4) Through the teachings of the Church

5) Through your friends

6) Through the circumstances of your life

7) Though rare, audibly

Pope Benedict XVI has also addressed this subject.[2]

It is vital we learn to listen to His voice, His whisper, every day.

---

[1] Lk 11:28

[2] See Zenit e-newsletter 2 March 2007, Pope Answers Seminarians, www.zenit.org for Pope Benedict VI's discussion of how God speaks to us; also cf *L'Osservatore Romano* n 9 28 February 2007

Under Christ's Lordship

In my own personal faith journey, I wish to pay tribute to my Protestant brothers and sisters in Christ whom I have encountered during ten years of involvement in ecumenical groups. Amongst them I witnessed wonderful examples of an earnest desire and active willingness to submit every part of one's life to Christ's headship. That in turn helped me to properly appreciate and make use of the channels of grace available to me through the teachings of the Catholic Church.

When we submit EVERY part of our lives to God; family, social, financial, health, welfare, faith and work, then EVERYTHING works in a better and more harmonious way.

In our marriages too, instead of using contraception, we are called to bring our marriages into conformity with God's will. Then the sanctifying graces and blessings of our marriage sacrament encounter no obstacle to be fully effective in our lives.[1]

A Hot Tip

Do you want a hot tip on how to maximise your happiness, strengthen your union, deepen your love, and increase your chances of staying together for life?

THEN ENSURE EVERY SINGLE MARITAL ACT THAT YOU EVER HAVE WITH YOUR SPOUSE IS OPEN TO CONCEIVING A CHILD!

In other words never, ever use contraception.

A Few Personal Recommendations

It is impossible to eliminate all the factors that contribute to marital break-up. The reasons for marital break-up are complex and often reach far back into the childhood and lives of one or both of the spouses.

Let me offer a few experiences from my own life. I stress they are NOT exhaustive, and I would remind you that I am no expert in marriage counselling. They are based on my own personal experience and observations, and they have helped me a lot. It may be that others have a different view or experience.

Anyhow, here goes:

- ✓ Individual personal prayer and prayer with your spouse every day is CRUCIAL.
- ✓ Read the scriptures and the teachings of the Catholic Church eg the Catechism
- ✓ No contraception – leave every marital act open to life and all the richness of marital dialogue entailed.

---

[1] cf CCn40; CCn110

- ✓ Use NFP to postpone pregnancy when circumstances are sufficiently serious.

- ✓ Tithe and give alms. Both are biblical concepts. The Old Testament indicates 10% of one's income to the Church, which some denominations and individuals take seriously. Whatever figure you decide, this giving acknowledges God as the source of all your resources.

- ✓ Go to Church at least on Sundays, with extra grace available at daily Mass!

- ✓ Explore together with the help of wise Christian counsel the subject of God's right order regarding headship and submission for husbands and wives in marriage.[1]

- ✓ Agree with your spouse on sound principles of child training, consistent discipline and character formation.

- ✓ Eliminate your viewing of immoral films, programmes, videos and literature.

- ✓ Reduce or eliminate secular TV.

- ✓ Seek spiritual direction if having difficultly communicating with each other. Therese and I attended a 'Marriage Encounter' weekend in March 2008, where we benefited greatly by learning skills to improve communication.[2]

Changeover From Contraception Not Easy

For those who have used contraception, the changeover is often not easy. Research has shown that the longer a couple has used contraception, the greater the struggle to fully embrace the chaste self-mastery required by a marriage open to life.[3] One husband expressed:

> *"to be perfectly honest, it doesn't always seem like it is worth the effort..."*

He then goes on to explain why he perseveres in exercising periodic self-mastery:

> *"...like most things in life that are hard, for instance marriage or raising children, it requires that you live outside yourself. It also requires that you give consideration to the larger implications of sexuality; it forces you to place your immediate choices in the context of spouse, children, family and Creator."* [4]

Contraception use essentially represents an unwillingness to exercise self-control. All of us however are called to exercise the virtue of chastity which:

---

[1] cf Ephesians 5 and CCn26-30
[2] see www.marriageencounter.ie or www.wwme.org
[3] cf Shivanandan p246
[4] cf Shivanandan p265-6

"...includes an apprenticeship in self-mastery which is a training in human freedom. The alternative is clear: either man governs his passions and finds peace, or he lets himself be dominated by them and becomes unhappy." [1]

Implore Divine Assistance

Pope Paul VI acknowledges the very real difficulties of marriage. He exhorts spouses to persevering prayer and the Eucharist as the source of charity and grace.[2]

He then encourages spouses to the grace of the Sacrament of Penance even in the face of failure:

"And if sin should still keep its hold over them, let them not be discouraged, but rather have recourse with humble perseverance to the mercy of God, which is poured forth in the sacrament of penance." [3]

Prayer, the Eucharist and the sacrament of penance are essential aids that assist us in the daily struggles of married life and indeed in all of life's struggles. Pope Pius XI reminds us to:

"Be subject to God... and your flesh [will be] subject to you.. [4]

He points out that it is impossible to overcome the 'flesh' by our own efforts alone without invoking God's grace.

A Word to Men

Men, if we buy sleazy newspapers in the morning and ogle over them in the workplace during the day, how do we expect to think of our wives respectfully when we come home in the evening?

Whether or not a man indulges in such a practice, I believe that some day, somewhere along the line, every married man meets his day of trial. A moment when temptation presents itself in its most enticing and suggestive form... the temptation to consider another woman, another choice, a relationship more attractive than his present one. I believe this happens to every married man without exception.

At that moment, a whole myriad of factors kick into place that will determine the outcome of the man's thought processes and choices. His family background, past experiences, strength of relationship with his wife, his level of convictions regarding fidelity to his marriage vows, the quality of his prayer life, the influence of social expectation, previous exposure to sexual images by pornography, impure literature, or TV and how he dealt with previous temptation all play a part.

---

[1] CCCn2339
[2] cfHVn25
[3] ibid
[4] cf CCn97-98

134

However, it is the 'strength-of-relationship-with-his-wife' factor where contraceptive practice plays its part. Contraception weakens marriage. In contraception, the other person becomes an object of pleasure and it starts to matter less who he or she is. The door to other possibilities is cracked open that little bit more.

God calls us men not to be slaves of our urges but to be HOLY! God calls us men - flesh, blood and guts men - as St. Padre Pio said, to do "violence to the sin in our lives", our minds, our hearts and in our attitudes to our wives and to any woman.

God is looking for men of valour, courage, heroism, purity, self-sacrifice, who each will have a reverential awe for that priceless treasure in his life... HIS WIFE.

Chapter Nineteen

The Choice Before Everyone

*"Seek the Lord all you, the humble
of the earth, who obey His commands.
Seek integrity, seek humility..."*

Zephaniah 2:3

The Choice is Yours

Obedience to the laws of Christ brings life, fulfilment and peace. Does the Catholic Church's teaching truly reflect the voice of Christ? Certainly it has been so in the experience of countless married couples who rejected contraception and found instead the way of truth shining through the teaching magisterium of the Church.

The teachings of the Church
are a signpost to salvation

It is only by following God's way that spouses will walk together in true love, unity and blessing. Only marital intercourse open to life is that which truly unites, truly strengthens, truly heals, truly fulfils, truly brings that lifelong spark to marriage. Any other sexual expression outside this God–ordained context steps beyond the parameters of God's will and will ultimately bring its own unhappiness and lack of fulfilment.

No matter how a scoffing world may try to obliterate it, the laws of God stamped into every man and woman can never be effaced.

The call to loving obedience to God and living "life to the full" that issues forth through Catholic teaching is none other than the call of the Gentle Healer, the Master of Love Himself who walked the earth 2000 years ago.

Many accepted Him and many rejected Him then, and today many do the same.

It is He who reminded us that the:

> *"...the gate is wide and the road is easy that leads to destruction and there are many who take it. For the gate is narrow and the road is hard that leads to life, and there are few who find it."* [1]

---

[1] cf Matt 7:13

We are told that in the end *"every knee shall bow and every tongue confess that Jesus Christ is Lord."* [1] On the road to salvation, towards the *"wedding feast of the lamb"*, [2] Christ shows the road and we are to follow. The teachings of the Church are a signpost to salvation.

Come and follow the Hero of all heroes, the Leader of all leaders, the Commander of all commanders, the Victor of all victors. We have to give Him our whole heart, and He will fill it with His own. We must leave aside the voices that would try to hold us back.

Come and join us; you won't be on your own.

I end this book by closing with a scripture which confronted me with a choice at a key time of decision in my life as a pharmacist. This choice I believe is laid before everyone using, advocating or promoting contraception:

*"See, I set before you
life or death,
blessing or curse.
Choose life that you and your
descendents might live."*

Deuteronomy 30:19

I pray that everyone who reads this verse will choose life.

---

[1] Phil 2:11
[2] cfRev 19:9

"[Christ]... the Spouse of the Church
now encounters Christian spouses
through the sacrament of matrimony.
Christ dwells with them, gives
them strength to take up their crosses
and so follow Him,
to rise again after they have fallen,
to forgive one another,
to bear one another's burdens,
to 'be subject to one another out
of reverence for Christ'
and to love one another with supernatural,
tender and fruitful love.
In the joys of their love and family life,
He gives them here on earth a foretaste
of the wedding feast of the Lamb."

Catechism of the Catholic Church n1642

This book, in its writing and effects,
is consecrated to the
Immaculate Heart of Mary.

Appendices

Appendix 1

Some Medical Facts

Contraceptive Pill Side-Effects

There is a dramatic increase in the risk of breast cancer, cervical cancer, deep vein thrombosis (blood clots) and other conditions reported with oral contraceptive pill use. Women who start the 'pill' before the age of 20 years are most at risk.

More information can be found in: *"A Consumer's Guide to the Pill and Other Drugs"* 3rd edition, ALL/National Book Store Inc, 2000 by Australian pharmacist John Wilks M.P.S., from which much of the below information was obtained.

Breast Cancer

✗ For women starting the 'pill' before the age of 20years, the risk of breast cancer was **170% - 480%** higher compared with healthy non-users of the same age, depending on the duration of use and study cited.[A,B,C,D]

✗ One of these studies reported a relative risk of dying by breast cancer of **820%** higher for those who started pill use before age 20years, compared to healthy non-users.[E]

✗ Women starting the pill between age 20-24 years had **three times** the risk of developing breast cancer before age 46 years compared to healthy non-users.[B]

✗ A massive **97%** of women in one study who had been diagnosed with invasive breast cancer before aged 36years had used oral contraception in the past.[F] Of all the women in this study – of all age groups – **85%** had used the pill at some time.[F]

✗ A startling result: even 3 months use of the pill has been reported to cause a **100%** increase in breast cancer.[G]

✗ For more than ten years use of the pill, breast cancer risk increased by **310%**.[H]

✗ Women starting pill use at an early age: " **have larger breast tumours...and a worse prognosis compared with later and never users** (of the pill) **with breast cancer**".[J]

Cervical Cancer

- Many studies reveal increased cervical cancer risks of **40-340%**, depending on first age of starting the 'pill' and the duration of use. A most serious risk **(280%)** exists for users aged less than 20years.[J,K,L,M]

- One study showed women who used the pill for only **1-6 months** had a **190%** increase in cervical cancer compared to non-users.[N]

- The pill activates and enhances the HPV (human papilloma virus) effect in triggering cervical cancer.[O,P]

Blood Clots (Deep Vein Thrombosis) (DVT)

- The commonly used so-called "second generation" oral contraceptive pills cause a **120-300%** increased risk of blood clots (DVT).[Q,R]

- Across all age groups, use of the 3rd generation pill brands (less commonly used since 1995 pill scare) had a **770%** greater blood clot risk than non-pill users.[S]

- For teenagers aged 15-19years using 3rd generation pill, risk of blood clots calculates to a **15-26 fold risk**, compared to non-users of the pill .[T]

- Between **30-50 fold** increased risk of blood clots for 3rd generation pill users who carry a blood-clotting factor V Leiden mutation[U,V] which occurs in 3-5% of European women.[W]

Infertility After Pill Use

- Some women may not conceive for up to 48 months or longer depending on their age.[X,Y]

Birth Defects

- Birth defects/chromosomal abnormalities can occur in children conceived right after the mother has ceased using the pill,[Z,AA] with one paper citing an incidence of such defects as increased by **400%**.[BB]

In Addition

As well as the above, the oral contraceptive pill is linked to stroke, pelvic inflammatory disease, ulcerative colitis, liver cell cancer, heart attacks, high blood pressure, depression, decreased libido, thrush and increased incidence of viral and bacterial infections in users (due to decreased immune response).

Medical Castration

Why has the pill gained such incredible popularity?   Perhaps an understanding can be obtained from the following statement of stunning honesty in the medical literature by Dr Arnold Klopper, shortly after the 'pill' was released on the world:

> "...the commercial interests backing these drugs have at their disposal a formidable machine of medical persuasion...women on oral contraceptives are, endocrinologically speaking, in a state of medical castration...to impose a 28-day cycle on such women is evidence of our adherence to social and lunar convention, not a physiologically necessity....The advertisement campaigns by which these compounds are made known to the medical public have been designed with great care in order to direct thought along desired lines. For example, words like testosterone have an unfortunate connotation and are carefully avoided...all but one of the compounds on the British market are (testosterone) derivatives. It is important to the sale of these drugs...that a fanciful resemblance to the physiological state of pregnancy is constantly stressed." *

Stage-Managed Marketing

Dr Klopper highlights some of the dynamics that have characterised the worldwide promotion of the pill. Despite the appalling side-effect profile of these products, the massive vested commercial interests, the carefully constructed PR, the artificially-induced 28 day cycle profiled to resemble the natural 'regular' cycle, the avoidance of linking pill hormones to testosterone, the carefully stage-managed perception of what is really a pill-induced state of castration, a truth kept from the consciousness of the consuming public.

The evidence that exists for the downplaying of the pill's side-effects by birth control advocates is startling.

Injustice to Women

Some family planning advocates defend or advocate use of the pill, citing a reported decrease in ovarian cancer rates (0.2% risk). The pill, pregnancy, and breast-feeding cause a cessation of ovulation giving a 'rest' to the ovaries, which is associated with a decreased incidence of ovarian cancer. To promote and emphasise this single effect as a 'selling point' for the pill while ignoring the magnitude of the side-effects documented above is either a woeful ignorance of the facts or a deliberate and cynical act of injustice to women.

---

* (Klopper, A., PhD, M.D., FRCOG, Advertisement and Classification of Oral Contraceptives, *British Medical Journal*, 1965, 2, 932-933. Used with permission from the *BMJ Publishing Group*)

References

A. Olsson H, Borg A, Ferno M, Moller TR, Ranstam J. Early oral contraceptive use and premenopausal breast cancer – a review of studies performed in South Sweden *Cancer Detection and Prevention* 1991:15 (4): 267, as cited by Wilks, J. MPS, A Consumer's Guide to the Pill and Other Drugs" 3rd edition, ALL/National Book Store Inc, 2000, p99

B. Olsson H, Olsson ML, Moller TR, Ranstam J, Holm P. *Lancet* (letter) 1985 March 30, 748-49, as cited by Wilks, J. MPS p101.

C. Olsson H, Moller TR, Ranstam J. Early oral contraceptive use and breast cancer among premenopausal women: Final report from a study in Southern Sweden. *Journal of the National Cancer Institute.* 1989;81(12):1000-4, as cited by Wilks, J. MPS p103

D. Johnson JH, Weighing the evidence on the pill and breast cancer *Family Planning Perspectives* 1989: 21 (2): 89-92, as cited by Wilks, J. MPS p101-102

E. Olsson H, Borg A, Ferno M, Moller TR, Ranstam J. Early oral contraceptive use and premenopausal breast cancer – a review of studies performed in South Sweden *Cancer Detection and Prevention* 1991:15 (4): 267, table IV as cited by Wilks, J. MPS p121

F. Rookus & Van Leeuwen. Oral Contraceptives and risk of Breast Cancer in women aged 20-54 years. *Lancet* 1994 ; 344; p844-51

G. Miller DR, Rosenberg L, et al Breast Cancer before age 45 and oral contraceptive use ; new findings. *American J of Epidemiology* 1989;129 (2):269- 80, as cited by Wilks, J. MPS p98

H. Miller , 1989 as above, as cited by Wilks, J. MPS p98

I. Olsson H, Borg A, Ferno M, Moller T, Ranstam J. Early oral contraceptive use and breast cancer in Southern Sweden. *Proc. Annu Meet Am Soc Clin Oncol.* 1989: A367, Ma, as cited by Wilks, J. MPS p120

J. Thomas DB, Ray RM. Oral contraceptives and invasive adenocarcinomas and adenosquamous carcinomas of the uterine cervix *Am J Epid* 1996;144:p284 table 2., as cited by Wilks, J. MPS p58

K. Kohler U, Wuttke P. results of a case control study of the current effect of various factors of cervical cancer risk . 2) Contraceptive behaviour and the smoking factor. *Zentralblatt fur gynakologie* 1994;116 (7): 405- 9 (Ma) , as cited by Wilks, J. MPS p54

L. Ursin G, Peters RK, Henderson BE, d'Ablaing G, Monroe KR, Pike MC. Oral contraceptive use and adenocarcinoma of cervix. *Lancet* 1994; 344; 1390-1394, as cited by Wilks, J. MPS p56-57

M. Brisson J et al Risk factors for cervical Intraepithelial Neoplasia: differences between low and high-grade lesions *American J of Epidemiology* 1994;140:700-710, as cited by Wilks, J. MPS p57-58

N. Ursin et al 1994 as above, as cited by Wilks, J. MPS p57

O. Chen Y-H, Huang L-H, Chen T-M. Differential effects of progestins and estrogens on long control regions of human papilloma virus types 16 and 18. *Biochemical and Biophysical Research Communications* 1996;224:p654, as cited by Wilks, J. MPS p75

P. Kenney JAW. Risk Factors associated with genital HPV infection. *Cancer Nurse* 1996 (Oct);19:5, p353, as cited by Wilks, J. MPS p77-78

Q. Bloemenkamp KW, Rosendal FR, Helmerhorst FM, Bauller HR, Vandenbroche JP. Enhancement by factor V Leiden mutation of deep vein thrombosis associated with oral contraceptives containing third generation progestogen. *Lancet* 1995;346:8990:1594, table 1, as cited by Wilks, J. MPS p150-151.

R. Spitzer WO, Lewis MA, Heineman LAJ et al. Third generation oral contraceptives and risk of venous thromboembolic disorders: an international case-control study *Br Med J* 1996;312:83-8, as cited by Wilks, J. MPS p153.

S. Bloemenkamp KW, Rosendal FR, Helmerhorst FM, Bauller HR, Vandenbroche JP. Enhancement by factor V Leiden mutation of deep vein thrombosis associated with oral contraceptives containing third generation progestogen. *Lancet* 1995;346:8990:1593-6, as cited by Wilks, J. MPS p150

T. Wilks, J. MPS, A Consumer's Guide to the Pill and Other Drugs" 3rd edition, ALL/National Book Store Inc, 2000, p151-152

U. Bloemenkamp et al p1593, as cited by Wilks, J. MPS p152

V. Vandenbrouke JP et al Increased risk of venous thrombosis in oral contraceptive users who are carriers of factor V Leiden mutation. *Lancet* 1994;344:p 1454, as cited by Wilks, J. MPS p145

W. as cited by Wilks, J. MPS p145

X. APPG 24th Ed Microgynon 30 monograph 1995 p1508, as cited by Wilks, J. MPS p189

Y. Micromedex vol 89 Oral contraceptives monograph, as cited by Wilks, J. MPS p190

Z. Wade ME, McCarthy PM et al. *Am J Obstet Gynaecol* 1995; 172: p698, as cited by Wilks, J. MPS p187

AA. Rahwan R, Prof Pharmacology & Toxicology, College of Pharmacy Ohio State University. *Chemical Contraceptives, Interceptives and Abortifacients* 1995, p32, as cited by Wilks, J. MPS p187-8

BB. Adverse Drug Reaction Bulletin, April 1984, no 105

Appendix 2

Do Contraceptive Pills Cause Abortion?

Chapter Six outlines how the process of conception occurs and raises the matter of the abortifacient nature of the pill. Here, the scientific evidence for this is examined.

According to pill manufacturer's information, one of the mode of actions of 'the Pill' is

> '...the rendering of the endometrium unreceptive to implantation' [a]

In other words, if, after intercourse, fertilisation has taken place and a new life has been conceived, the newly-formed developing embryo is prevented from implanting in its mother's womb (endometrium or uterus).

EVERY CHEMICAL CONTRACEPTIVE PREPARATION INVOLVING PILLS, INJECTIONS, IMPLANTS AND INTRAUTERINE DEVICES INHERENTLY EMPLOYS THIS MECHANISM AS PART OF ITS OVERALL MODE OF ACTION.

This background action is always present on any given cycle.

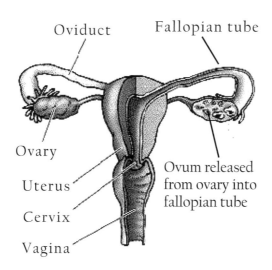

The Process of
Human Conception

There are three other principal ways in which the Pill and other contraceptive drugs work:

a) By prevention of ovulation (suppression of ovum release from the ovary).

b) There is thickening of cervical mucus (at cervix) which makes it difficult for the sperm to reach the ovum.

c) There is decreased muscular action of the fallopian tubes thereby slowing transportation of the ovum to the womb.

Only with the complete suppression of ovulation on every occasion could any product be considered to be truly contraceptive (i.e. contra-conceptive). In practice this is not the case. As seen in Table 1 below, the range of ovulation occurring during use of contraceptive products is significant, varying widely (0 to 100%) depending on the type of preparation used.

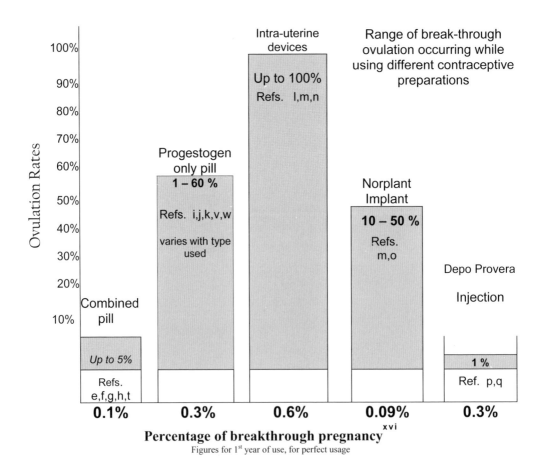

Percentage of breakthrough pregnancy[xvi]

Figures for 1st year of use, for perfect usage

Table 1

When such 'breakthrough ovulation' occurs during contraceptive use, an ovum is present that is available for potential fertilisation (conception). Should conception occur, a human embryo is thus present for possible implantation.

The question arises as to what degree are such embryos lost during contraceptive use because of this action of contraceptive drugs at the endometrium level.

Medical literature suggests that this embryo-losing mode of action does indeed occur to some degree. [d,e,t]

That this endometrial mechanism is operative at all means that, by medical definition, 'the pill' is intrinsically abortifacient [b,c] in nature. In other words, it causes an early abortion just after fertilisation. Several authors have highlighted the abortion causing consequences of using the Pill. [d,t,u]

What Loss of Embryos?

Sometimes an identifiable, established pregnancy occurs during contraceptive use. Such pregnancies appear to happen even during correct usage of the contraceptive pill, i.e. even when women faithfully remember to take their contraceptive doses at the appropriate time.[p,r]

The very fact that break-through pregnancies happen at all confirms the reality of ovulation and subsequent fertilisation during contraceptive drug use.

Stress, disease, infection, irregular Pill use, vomiting, diarrhoea, and the use of several types of drug can all add to the possibility of such break-through pregnancy by lowering the efficiency of the contraceptive in use.

It is hard to quantify just how many embryos are lost through the abortifacient action of contraceptives at the implantation stage but it has been estimated that a silent chemical abortion happens once in about 200 menstrual cycles for a woman continually on the combined Pill.[s]

The fact that millions of women use these contraceptive methods implies that these chemical abortions must run into millions worldwide.

Misleading Information

It is virtually certain that chemical abortions occur at the pre-implantive stage during contraceptive drug use. The fact that such abortions occur at all is morally unacceptable but more especially in a product which is purported to avoid conception.

Information supplied to users relating to the effect of contraceptives is misleading. Many women, believing that they are using a preparation to avoid conception are likely to have been unwittingly involved in the loss of their own children through early abortion at the pre-implantive stage.

Moral Implications for Professional Providers.

The fact that Pill information leaflets either exclude information on the abortifacient nature of the drug, or couch information in such technical terminology which only a trained professional could understand, raises serious issues of informed consent. Clear moral and ethical implications arise for healthcare professionals who provide these contraceptives to women not suspecting such an action, and the public in general.[t,u]

References

a) www.emc.medicines.org.uk Femodene, Product Characteristics, section 5:1 as of 13 Feb. 09; also ABPI Data Sheet Compendium. Datapharm Publications Ltd. 1996-1997 (Femodene) p1007.

b) Stedmans Medical Dictionary 26th ed. William and Wilkins, London 1995.

c) Blakistons Gould Medical Dictionary 4th ed. New York 1979.

d) Somkuti, S.G., Fritz, M. et al. The effect of oral contraceptive pills on markers of endometrical receptivity. *Fertility and Sterility*, 65(3) Mar 1996, pp 484-488.

e) Van der Vange, N. Ovarian activity during low dose oral contraceptives. *Contemporary Obstetrics and Gynaecology*. Editor: Chamberlain, G., Butterworths, London, 1988, pp319-326.

f) Grimes, D., Godwin, A., et al. Ovulation and follicular development associated with three low dose oral contraceptives: A randomised controlled trial. *Obstetrics and Gynaecology*, 83, (1) 1994, pp29-34.

g) Westcombe . R., Ellis, R. and Fotherby, K. Suppression of ovulation in women using a triphasic oral contraceptive. *British Journal of Family Planning*, 13, 1987, pp 127-132.

h) Ehmann, R., "Abortifacient Contraception – The Pharmaceutical Holocaust". Human Life International, Ontario, 1993, pp7-16.

i) Langren, B.M. and Diczfalusy, E., Hormonal effects of the300ug norethisteone (NET) minipill. Contraception, 21, 1980, pp87-99.

j) Neal,, M.J., Medical Pharmacology at a glance. Blackwell Scientific Publications, London, 1991, p67.

k) Belfield, T., Contraceptive Handbook, 3rd ed. Family Planning Association, London, 1992, p37.

l) Zatuchi, G. and Goldsmith, A., Long term Clinical experience with levo-norgestrel-releasing IUD. *Intra-uterine Contraception*. Harper and Row, Philadelphia, 1987, pp232-237.

m) Croxatto , H.B Diaz, S. et al. Plasma progesterone levels during long term treatment with levo-norgestrel and Copper IUD comparative trail. *Contraception* 49, 1994, pp 56-72.

n) Andersson et al ., L-norgestrel and Copper IUD comparative trial. *Contraception* ,49, 1994,pp56-72.

o) Shaoban, M.M. et al., Sonographic assessment of ovarian and endometrial changes during long-term Norplant use and their correlation with hormone levels. *Fertility and Sterility*, 59(5), 1993, pp998-1002.

p) Hatcher, R.A., Trussell, J .et al. Contraceptive Technology 16th ed. Irvington Publishers, New York, 1994, pp637-687.

q) Pardthaisong, T., Grey. R., In utero exposure to steroid contraceptives and outcome of pregnancy. *American Journal of Epidemiology*, 134,(8), 15 Oct.1991 pp795-803.

r) Duncan, G., Harper, C. et al., Termination of pregnancy; lessons for prevention. *British Journal of Family Planning*, 15, 1990, pp 112-117.

s) Kuhar, B.M. PhD Abortifacient Drugs and Devices; Do the numbers add up?, published in;Infant Homicides through Contraceptives,, Eternal Life publishers, KY, USA, 1995, p26,

t) Larimore, L, Stanford, J. Postfertilisation effects of oral contraceptives and their relationship to informed consent. *Archives of Family Medicine*, 9, Feb 2000 pp126-133

u) Larimore, W The abortifacient effect of the Birth Control Pill and the principle of 'double-effect' *Ethics and Medicine* 16:1 2000, pp23-30

v) Cerazette Data Sheet www.emc.medicines.co.uk 1% ovulation reported as of 13 Sept 2007

w) Cerazette allows 3-9% ovulation. See Chardy C.k. Dept G.U. Medicine, Coventry and Warkickshire Hospital, UK http://www.sexualhealthmatters.com/v6iss4/article3.html

Appendix 3

Contraceptive Usage Leads to Widescale Abortion

Statistics reveal that the majority of babies killed by surgical abortion were conceived during contraceptive intercourse. In other words contraceptive use leads to more abortion, contrary to what we are so often told.

Study 1: 52-70% (depending on age) of women obtaining abortion used contraception at the time of conception.

(Addlestone GR, BPAS News Sept 1985)

Study 2: 56% of women obtaining abortions used contraception at the time of conception.

(Duncan et al, British J Family Planning, 1990 (15) 112-117)

Study 3: 54% women obtaining abortions were using contraception at the time of conception.

(Bromham DR, Cartmill RSV, British J Family Planning 1993, 19: 179-183)

Study 4: 61 % women obtaining abortions were using contraception at the time of conception.

(New Zealand Medical Journal 25 May 1994.)

Study 5: 58% women obtaining abortions used contraception at the time of conception.

(Henshaw SK, Kost K, Family Planning Perspectives Vol 28 (14) July/Aug 96)

Not without reason does Pope John Paul II state that:

> "*Indeed, the pro-abortion culture is especially strong precisely where the Church's teaching on contraception is rejected.*"

(Evangelium vitae n13).

From a further secular source we have confirmation of the contraception–abortion link. Christopher Tietze, one of the world's most experienced abortion statisticians, confirmed that one can expect a high correlation between abortion and contraception in populations to which both contraception and abortion are available.

He writes that women who have practiced contraception are more likely to have had abortions than those who have not practiced contraception, and women who have had abortions are more likely to have been contraceptors than women without a history of abortion. (cf "Abortion and Contraception." In *Abortion: Readings and Research* Toronto: Butterworth & Co., 1981, pages 54 to 60)

Appendix 4

Breastfeeding's Effect on the Spacing of Births

Some studies conducted by the Couple to Couple League found that mothers who followed the rules of so-called 'ecological breastfeeding' averaged 14.5 months before returning to fertility after childbirth.

This type of breastfeeding, used by mothers for centuries before bottle feeding, can be summarised by the following seven points, as compiled by the Couple to Couple League. (Kippley, Art of NFP p345).

1. Exclusive breastfeeding for the first six months; no other liquids or solids.
2. No bottles or pacifiers (dummies) used.
3. Pacify your baby by allowing it to suckle.
4. Sleep with your baby for night feedings.
5. Sleep with your baby for a daily-nap feeding.
6. Nurse frequently day and night, and avoid schedules. Nurse on demand.
7. Avoid any practice that restricts nursing or separates you from your baby.

Scientifically speaking, it is the frequency of sucking around the clock that is the single most important factor in postponing the return of fertility after childbirth.

A fascinating discussion of this type of breastfeeding and of mother-child bonding and its effect on deferring the return of fertility post child-birth, are found in this book on NFP.

Appendix 5

Some Relevant Questions

What about VERY serious reasons where conception must be absolutely avoided?

Pope Pius XII observes that there can arise situations in which the risk of motherhood cannot be run or must be avoided completely. There can be such circumstances, he acknowledges, where observing the infertile periods as in NFP:

"either does not give sufficient security or must be rejected for other reasons."

In such an instance, he continues, complete abstinence is the only moral response even to levels of heroism some may not have thought possible. Such heroism is indeed possible by:

"sincerely and perseveringly seeking divine help."

He adds that, in such an instance:

"It would be a wrong towards men and women of our age to judge them incapable of continuous heroism."

Pope Pius XII warns:

"It is clear; he who does not want to master himself is not able to do so, and he who wishes to master himself relying on his own powers, without sincerely and perseveringly seeking divine help, will be miserably deceived." [1]

Can someone using contraception receive the Eucharist?

Receiving the Eucharist is an outward expression of intimate communion with Jesus Christ. It acknowledges assent to His Gospel and the teachings of His Church. Christ loves His people so much that he left Himself on earth in the Holy Eucharist. The Mass is *"the sacred banquet of communion with the Lord's body and blood".*[2] It is wholly directed toward the *"intimate union of the faithful with Christ through communion".*[3] In other words, Christ desires union with His people.

---

[1] cf Allocution to Midwives 1951
[2] CCCn1382
[3] CCCn1382

Grave sin deprives us of true communion with God as well as the serious risk of excluding us from eternal life with God in His Kingdom.[1] The use of contraception falls into the category of grave sin.[2]

We are reminded of a *"specific moral duty incumbent upon Christians who wish to participate fully in the Eucharist"* -to keep intact the "invisible bonds" of *"true communion with the Father, the Son and the Holy Spirit"*. In the context of receiving the Eucharist *"in a worthy manner"* Pope John Paul II quotes:

> *"Anyone conscious of grave sin must receive the sacrament of reconciliation before coming to communion."* [3]

Can use of contraception, or sterilisation, from the day of marriage invalidate the marriage?

Canon Law outlines the conditions and the impediments to validity of a marriage.[4] The Catechism states that:

> *"Unity, indissolubility and openness to fertility are essential to marriage."* [5]

It is to these three essential elements that spouses consent at the altar. If, in declaring their consent, one of the spouses excluded by a positive act of the will one of these essential elements, the marriage is not valid.[6]

The free exchange of consent of the spouses at the altar in the form prescribed by the Church institutes the sacrament and subsequent consummation completes it.

If a couple exchange public consent, but have the firm intention to avoid permanently having children by using contraception or any other means, the marriage is invalid. There is of course the scenario outlined earlier in this book of the couple who, for really serious reasons, using moral means, may postpone having a child for an indeterminate time, even if that period were to become permanent. In any scenario, it is the intent of the couple that is the crucial consideration.

For example, Pope Pius XII outlines how if one spouse enters marriage with the intent to restrict exercise of the marital act solely to the natural infertile periods of the woman's monthly cycle without serious reason and against the other spouse's will, this:

> *"...would imply an essential defect in the marriage consent, which would result in the marriage being invalid."* [7]

---

[1] cf CCCn1472

[2] cf CCn56

[3] Ecclesia de Eucharistia, Encyclical, Pope John Paul II 17 April 2003, n36; CCCn1385

[4] CIC n1055-1165

[5] CCCn1664

[6] cf CICn1101

[7] Allocution to Midwives 1951

Similarly, if another couple of fertile age get married and one of them had been permanently, deliberately surgically sterilised for birth control purposes prior to the marriage, with no intention of ever attempting to reverse it, then that party has withheld proper consent regarding openness to fertility. In such an instance, such a couple are not truly married.

It may arise that some spouses publicly declare their consent at the altar, intending to use contraception from that night until such time at a later date they feel 'ready' for children. Whilst such a marriage is valid such a practice contradicts the ends and purposes of marriage. How can such a couple expect the grace of the sacrament to flow freely through their marriage? How can they expect the power of Christ and His Holy Spirit to act in their union? How can they hope to bear the spiritual fruits appropriate to the marriage sacrament?

What will be the effect of this on their marriage until such time as they consummate their marriage without the use of contraception, coupled with an openness to life? Only then can they enter into a truly 'one-flesh' union.

A marriage is not valid if a couple intend to use contraception permanently for all their married lives, having no intention of ever having a child.

It is the intention of the couple that has an influential effect on whether the purposes, the ends and the meaning of marriage are properly fulfilled in the moral sense. While couples are often sincere in their intent, the means used must always be in accordance with the moral law.

What about theologians who lead spouses into error?

In 1987, Pope John Paul II addressed the matter of theologians who cast doubt and dissent within the Christian community on the Church's teaching on contraception:

> "A grave responsibility derives from this; those who place themselves in open conflict with the law of God authentically taught by the Church, guide spouses along a false path. The Church's teaching on contraception does not belong to the category of matter open to free discussion among theologians. Teaching the contrary amounts to leading the moral consciences of spouses into error."[1]

What about Priests who teach it is OK to use contraception?

Poor advice from priests is something that unfortunately I have encountered in my own personal search for the truth on the subject of contraception. Indeed, several of my pharmacist peers, troubled by qualms of doubt and questioning, received advice to 'follow your conscience' and 'do as you will' from priests they consulted. Yes, we all must follow our conscience, but our consciences must be fully informed. Pius XI spoke very directly to priests on the matter of giving guidance on this very subject:

---

[1] Pope John Paul II, 6 July 1987, cf Kippley, SMC p140

> *"We admonish, therefore, priests who hear confessions and others who have care of souls...not to allow the faithful entrusted to them to err regarding this most grave law of God; much more, that they keep themselves immune from such false opinions, in no way conniving in them.*
>
> *If any confessor or pastor of souls, who, may God forbid, lead the faithful entrusted to him into these errors or should at least confirm them by approval or by guilty silence, let him be mindful of the fact that he must render a strict account to God, the Supreme judge, for the betrayal of his sacred trust, and let him take to himself the words of Christ: "They are blind and leaders of the blind, and if the blind lead the blind, both fall into the pit."* [1]

To act with correct authority, anyone speaking in the name of the Church must give guidance according to the mind of the Church, not his own mind.

What about sterilisation?

A few years ago, a well known media personality in Ireland boasted on radio about his sterilisation. Some time later, it was reported that his marriage had broken up. Just recently two doctors told me, amongst those patients who underwent a sterilisation procedure, they noticed a pattern of marital breakdown two years later. What effects can sterilisation have on a marriage and on the Divine plan for marriage?

Exactly the same principles apply to sterilisation as to contraception except that sterilisation is a surgical version that is more difficult to reverse. Reversal of sterilisation is possible and there are some physicians who specialise in this procedure. Drawing from the sources cited in this book, here are the principal considerations:

1. In sterilisation or contraception, the marital act is no longer a proper spousal union.

2. Spouses deprive themselves of the powerful benefits which flow into their marriage by leaving their marriage open to life.

3. The marital act is denied its inherent procreative power, resulting in a violation of the true nature and interior order of the act. [2]

4. In a sterilised or contraceptive marital act, there is no longer a total giving of self. The sterilised person can no longer be totally received by the other because they are not giving of their whole self. In this sense, there can no longer be a true act of conjugal love.

---

[1] CCn57

[2] cfTOBp398

160

5. Sterilisation, or contraception, falsifies the language of total self-giving that is being expressed by the body. In this sense, the total physical self-giving being expressed becomes a lie.[1]

6. Both the spouses and their sexuality are degraded and manipulated.[2]

7. Sterilisation, or contraception, turns marriage away from its 'supreme' gift of a child. *"...refusal of fertility turns marriage away from its "supreme" gift, the child."* [3]

8. Pleasure becomes a predominant principle. The spouses depart from authentically loving each other as persons and instead move towards a state where they become as objects to be enjoyed. In this scenario it is wives who tend to become the most used and abused.

9. A contraceptive or sterilised couple deprive themselves of the marriage strengthening effect of the presence of children.

10. The children who are born may wonder about the brothers and sisters they will never meet. They are also left to make sense of the perspective: "I am lucky to be alive. I happened to be born when my parents wanted a child" or "Am I a mistake? Did they really want me?"

11. Every contraceptive or sterilised act is an act which contradicts the inherent meaning of the words of the marriage vows: "I take you as my husband...I take you as my wife". In such a scenario, there is no longer a giving or receiving of the whole person.

12. By thwarting the birth of even one child by sterilisation or contraception - a child who had been planned in the mind of God as a gift to a marriage - an entire bloodline that was destined to exist can be wiped out. Countless future descendants who were destined for life on earth are stopped from coming into existence.

13. Failed contraception or failed sterilisation increases the likelihood of abortion.[4]

Those who have had a sterilisation procedure have a responsibility to ascertain if their procedure is reversible. If so, they have a serious obligation to undergo the necessary surgery to reverse it, if possible. For further information on

---

[1] cfFCn32
[2] cfFCn32
[3] CCCn1664; GSn50
[4] see appendix 3

exploring the matter of sterilisation reversal see relevant section at website www.omsoul.com.

What's the 'Correct Focus' for husband and wife during the marital act?

This is an important question and one that John Paul II gave some attention to in his book *Love and Responsibility*. In the minds and hearts of each spouse, each marital act must first and foremost be an interpersonal act of betrothed love.

During the marital act, the attention of each spouse *"must be fixed on the other, upon his or her true good"* - the 'good' of the 'other' person must be the principal focus. The act *"should be an expression of love with pleasure as the incidental accompaniment of the sexual act."* [1] Neither the pursuit of pleasure nor the goal of having a child are to be the principal conscious focus for spouses in the marital act.

As a point of interest, I know couples who had difficulties conceiving and the more they concentrated on conceiving, the more frustrated and disillusioned they became. However, when they decided to relax and enjoy one another in their marital union, and leave any thought of conception aside, they conceived soon thereafter.

To maintain this focus of 'person' before all else is a safeguard against the ever present tendency to allow the other person to become an object of pleasure, where they are used rather than cherished. This is something *every* marriage has to guard against. [2] Such use of the other degrades the act of mutual love between persons to a so-called utilitarian level, which inevitably is what happens when procreation is excluded from the marital act (as in contraception). [3]

In every act, the perspective that each is a gift to the other must be safeguarded. [4] The other person can never be a means to an end.

What about newly married couples postponing children?

What about a newly married couple who have decided – even before they get married - to postpone children for a few years while they dedicate their time and energy to other aspects of life or intend to strengthen their newly founded relationship? Is this respecting the true purpose of marriage?

A couple should not try to avoid conception if they have no *SERIOUS* reason to do so. As Fr Paul Marx once said: "If you're not ready to have children, you are not ready to get married". The two primary ends of marriage are 1) unity of the spouses and 2) the procreation and education of children. The two go hand in hand. The essence of marriage is unity, indissolubility and openness to fertility.

---

[1] cf LR p234-5
[2] cf LR p225
[3] cf LR p225;234
[4] cf LF n12

This is what spouses consent to when they get married. The mission of every married couple should be to have children. It is their specific calling.

A couple called to marriage enter a union where God asks them to participate in His power of creation and generation of children. They are to seek God's will for their fertility amidst the particular and unique circumstances of their lives, guided by the principles of 'responsible parenthood' outlined by the Church. As we saw earlier, the Church doesn't spell out what constitutes serious reasons. That's for each couple to discern in good conscience according to their own circumstances. The responsibility to do so properly however, does rest with them. We are called to be co-operators with God's plan, not controllers of it.

How 'serious' or 'grave' are a couple's reasons for postponing a child now that they are married? Are they serious enough to deprive the newly married couple of the 'supreme gift' of a child – the 'crowning glory' of their marriage? How much have they prayed to discern God's will as to His intentions for the family? Is it possible that God called them to be married and then from the outset asked them to delay having children?

The arrival of children is a strengthening factor in a marriage, a dimension many couples deprive themselves of by their decision to postpone the arrival of any children. Are their reasons serious enough to deprive their marriage of the strengthening bonds that a child brings? Could it be that spurious reasons thwart God's plan to bless them with a child shortly after being married? Spouses are the stewards of a wonderful privilege and a great responsibility. Husband and wife have been elevated to the privilege of being co-operators with the creative power of God in the generation of new life. It is to this they consented when they exchanged their marriage vows.

How can such a couple presume that they will have a child when <u>they</u> are ready? Have they really thought through the reasons for them getting married in the first place? If they were getting married to deliberately postpone having children, why did they not postpone getting married?

Even for such couples who use moral means such as NFP to postpone a child, are they conforming their activity to the 'creative intention of God' for marriage as outlined in the following passage:

> "In the task of transmitting life, therefore, they are not free to proceed completely at will, as if they could determine in a wholly autonomous way the honest path to follow; but they must conform their activity to the creative intention of God, expressed in the very nature of marriage and of its acts, and manifested by the constant teaching of the Church." [1]

This raises the question to prospective spouses about why they are getting married in the first place if they are not open to having children right away (in the absence of serious circumstances)?

---

[1] HVn10

Such a couple could find themselves in the scenario outlined by Pope Pius XII, where to enter marriage and to use NFP 'always and deliberately' with no 'serious' or 'grave' reason *"would be a sin against the very meaning of conjugal life."* [1]

What about doctors, pharmacists and condom promoters?

Doctors, pharmacists and other healthcare professionals allow their esteemed professions to act as vehicles for contraceptive provision. In light of the evidence and information in this book, what's the position - morally, ethically and socially - of Catholic doctors and pharmacists who prescribe or dispense contraceptive products?

In an address to Catholic Italian pharmacists in 1994, Pope John Paul II stated:

"One cannot accept being party to attacks on life...or on procreation." [2]

Speaking to pharmacists on 29th October 2007, Pope Benedict XVI stated that:

"we cannot anaesthetize consciences as regards, for example the effects of certain molecules that have the goal of preventing the implantation of the embryo or shortening a person's life." [3]

In handling contraceptive or abortifacient drugs, some healthcare professionals argue that their professional code of ethics permits or even compels them to participate in such promotion. It is sometimes argued that a healthcare professional cannot impose his private views on others. It is also argued that to be 'professional' means that healthcare workers must supply all drug products required. Pharmacists and doctors, it is said, should stick to the scientific facts of how contraceptive drugs work and not stray into the moral arena.

However, we are reminded that:

"Each individual in fact has moral responsibility for the acts he personally performs; no-one can be exempted from this responsibility and on the basis of it everyone will be judged by God himself." [4]

There is an ethical code higher than a profession's official code of ethics that calls upon a greater loyalty should there be a conflict between the two.

Healthcare professionals are not like robots merely fulfilling a technical function in a moral vacuum. We humans are physical, mental, spiritual and moral beings. Our actions affect the welfare of others. Every one of us has a duty of care to our fellow human beings.

---

[1] Pius XII, 1951, in Smith, p 454
[2] *L'Osservatore Romano*, English Weekly Edition, No. 6, 9 February 1994, Rome
[3] Pope Benedict XVI, 25th International Congress of Catholic Pharmacists, 29th October 2007, Rome
[4] Pope John Paul II cfEVn74

In his encyclical letter *Evangelium Vitae* Pope John Paul II stated that:

> "*Whoever attacks human life in some way attacks God himself.*" [1]

Attacking God is not an enviable place for anyone to be.

This raises serious questions for those involved in propagating contraception.

The vast majority of healthcare professionals are hard working, sincere, work under pressurised conditions and seek to act in the best interests of their patients. They find themselves in many professional-related scenarios not of their making, often faced with tough ethical and moral dilemmas. Most wish to make the right decisions.

Contraceptive promotion encroaches onto sacred ground. It enters the very essence of marriage, procreation, the sanctity of life and spousal relationships. In dealing with procreation every man is called to act with the most profound reverence and stewardship according to his station.

The vast majority of healthcare workers I believe, if they sincerely think it through, have no desire to be in a position where they are party to attacks on life, procreation, even God Himself. Most pharmacists and healthcare professionals I know are genuine, honest, want to do a good job and provide for their families and loved ones. Indeed several newly qualified pharmacists have contacted me when they have had to deal with this dilemma face to face. They want to do 'the right thing' but find themselves under immense pressure to conform.

This is a matter that requires much wider airing and discussion. Pharmacists worldwide are vigorously contesting the right to conscientious objection in practice. [2]

What about the children at embryonic stage lost with abortifacient contraceptives?

Unknown millions of embryos are lost every year around the world by the use of contraceptive pills and drugs. The loss of human life is staggering. What is certain is that every single one of these human embryos is known to God. The life of every human being is sacred and is to be treated as a person right from the moment of conception. [3]

We each have a duty of care to every other human being: "*Every man is his "brother's keeper" because God entrusts us to one another.*" [4] We are also accountable for our care of others: "*From man, with respect to his fellow man, I will demand an accounting.*" [5]

---

[1] EVn9

[2] cf www.pfli.org

[3] cf EVn60; EVn61

[4] EVn19

[5] EVn38; cf Gen 9:5

The Psalmist addressing God said:

> "You created every part of me; you put me together in my mother's womb... The days allotted to me had all been recorded in your book before any of them ever began." [1]

Scripture indicates the mystery of God's plan for men and women yet to be born long before they are brought into physical existence. How much has God's plan for the human race been thwarted by contraception across the earth?

What About Infertile Couples?

Infertility is a heartbreak for many couples who would love to have children. I know several such couples who cannot have children. Yet their marriages are loving, united and bear much fruit in the lives of those around them. One lady wrote:

> "Two years after we married, my husband and I were told after hospital tests that we both had 'unexplainable infertility'. We were offered IVF (in vitro fertilisation) which, because of our Catholic faith, we declined. We both didn't want a child at the expense of lost or destroyed embryos / children as happens in IVF.
>
> I left full-time work to do pro-life talks in schools, crisis pregnancy counselling, post abortion healing ministries and Legion of Mary work. We continued to hope and pray that if it was God's will, He would bless us with a family. Four years later, at age 42, we started the long process of trying to adopt a child from abroad. We are still waiting for the gift of a child.
>
> I rejoice that God has blessed me with lots of "spiritual children" through my Legion of Mary work and pro-life work. WOW.
>
> I accept the possibility that we may never have physical children. But more important to me is that every day we thank God for the blessings of our marriage and that we realise and accept that love is sacrificial. We are sometimes sorrowful that we don't have physical children but we both want to do God's will first and foremost because only in His will is there true fulfilment and happiness.
>
> Anyhow, raising, encouraging, loving and caring for spiritual children is a full time job!!!" [2]

This lady has truly embraced 'the cross' of infertility and has brought an enormous amount of good out of it. The Church has a special mention for couples suffering with infertility:

---

[1] Ps139:13;16
[2] MM Personal communication 22 August 2007

"Spouses who suffer from infertility after exhausting legitimate medical procedures should unite themselves with the Lord's Cross, the source of all spiritual fecundity. They can give expression to their generosity by adopting abandoned children or performing demanding services for others." [1]

In infertility, the true symbolism of the spouses' marital acts is not diminished by their inability to conceive. True love and true union are still fully expressed. Just because they cannot have children does not mean their love cannot be fruitful.

There has been remarkable success, however, for infertile couples using a new type of infertility treatment called Natural Procreative (NaPro) technology. It is non-invasive and harnesses the natural conditions of fertility. It addresses hormonal imbalance and is completely morally legitimate. It has achieved success rates greater than *in vitro fertilisation*. It has also been greatly effective in the treatment of recurrent miscarriage. [2]

This organization has pioneered remarkably successful infertility treatment, and fertility healthcare, in keeping with correct moral principles. It has trained practitioners working in several countries of the world.

Is contraception an ideological tool?

As mentioned in Chapter Eleven, most couples using contraception are oblivious to the fact that they are unsuspecting pawns in an ideological culture war. They do not realise they are using a product steeped in ideological significance and promoted nationally and globally with almost religious fervour by its proponents. As mentioned at the beginning of this book, the propagation of contraception was originally designed to undermine the authority of the Christian denominations.

On a global level at the United Nations, the agencies promoting contraception are the self same ones who are promoting abortion. They are the same agencies which downgrade marriage between husband and wife and erode the traditional family as the fundamental unit of society. [3]

Contraception is a cornerstone tool of that ideological worldview which Pope John Paul II has termed the "Culture of Death"; a culture in direct conflict with what he calls the "Culture of Life" and the "Gospel of Life". The future of love, marriage, family, Church and even mankind itself is at stake.

What is to be the outcome of this dramatic worldwide, even cosmic clash of belief systems? Only one will win out in the end. Pope John Paul II expressed his conviction:

"...of the absolute certitude that in God's plan, life will be victorious. "And death will be no more." [4]

The *"blood of Christ"*, he says, *"is the foundation"* for this certainty.

---

[1] CCCn2379

[2] More information can be had from the Pope Paul VI Institute at <u>www.popepaulvi.com</u>

[3] cf*The Gender Agenda*, Dale O'Leary, Vital Issues Press, 1997

[4] Rev21:4, EVn25

There we have it. It's absolutely certain. Life WILL win over death, good WILL win over evil, blessing WILL win over curse. I know which side I want to be on!

> Most couples using contraception are oblivious to the fact that they are unsuspecting pawns in an ideological culture war.

Appendix 6

A Quick Reference on Contraception and NFP

In the terminology used by the Church, contraceptive use:

✦ Causes the total physical self-giving of the marital act to become a lie (FCn11)

✦ Causes spouses to claim a power that belongs solely to God (cf John Paul II, Oct 10th 1983)

✦ Degrades and manipulates human sexuality (cfFCn32)

✦ Degrades and manipulates the spouses performing the act (cfFCn32)

✦ Causes the marital act to cease being an act of love (cfTOBp398)

✦ Falsifies the 'inner truth' of marital love (cfFCn32)

✦ Frustrates the natural procreative power and purpose of the marital act (cf CCn54)

✦ Violates the 'interior order' of marital union (cfTOBp398)

✦ Is intrinsically evil (cfCCCn2370)

✦ Is a grave sin (CCn56)

Contraceptive use:

✗ creates a barrier between the spouses.

✗ creates a barrier between the spouses and God.

✗ prevents true conjugal one-flesh union.

✗ changes the focus to self rather than on the other person.

✗ causes a disintegration of intimacy and true communication between spouses.

✗ Is a root of marital strife.

✗ opposes the unifying, sanctifying grace of the marriage sacrament.

✗ robs spouses of the blessings of children - the supreme gift of marriage.

✗ constitutes a revolt against God's plan for marriage.

✗ opposes the 'proper mission' of a married couple.

✗ means the marital act no longer expresses true marital love.

✗   undermines true manhood and womanhood. It denies men the opportunity of being real, self - sacrificial, responsible, Christian men.

✗   facilitates the abuse of women.

✗   causes the 'person' to become an 'object' of pleasure.

✗   causes the death of human embryos at conception by the pill and other abortifacient products.

NFP – A Summary

Natural family planning, conducted with the right intent, and in appropriate circumstances:

✓   Respects the divine law.

✓   Respects the order of nature.

✓   Respects the truth and the interior order of the marital act.

✓   Allows each marital act to remain open to life.

✓   Upholds the dignity of the person.

✓   Allows the total giving of self as a gift.

✓   Does not impede development of the natural processes.

✓   Does not falsify the language of total self-giving.

✓   Helps drive out selfishness (HVn21).

✓   Develops the personality of each spouse (HVn21).

✓   Enriches the spiritual values of the spouses (HVn21).

✓   Enables an efficacious influence of the parents on their children (HV21).

✓   Can be used in grave circumstances to postpone birth.

✓   Financially costs nothing.

✓   Does not render the woman permanently infertile.

Natural family planning, when justified, allows marriage to be enriched through the abstinence, shared responsibility, mutual respect, increased self-mastery and the intimate communication entailed.

Appendix 7

NFP Websites

Creighton Method   www.popepaulvi.com
In Ireland   www.fertilitycare.net   Tel: +353 91 720055

Billings Ovulation Method   www.woomb.org
Billings Ireland www.naomi.ie   Tel: +353 1 8786156

Human Life International   www.hli.org
Human Life International (Ireland) www.hliireland.ie

Couple to Couple League   www.ccli.org

One More Soul www.omsoul.com

Family of the Americas   www.familyplanning.net

Christian website   www.sweeterthanhoney.org

Appendix 8

Questions for you!

Having read this book on contraception, how would you answer the following questions?

In a contraceptive marriage:

? Are spouses being faithful to their marriage vows when they use contraception?

? Is God still truly welcomed at the heart of their marriage?

? Can the grace of their sacrament still flow freely?

? In the marital act, are husband and wife loving each other in a total self-giving?

? Are they truly united in 'one flesh' union during contraceptive intercourse?

? Is a marriage strengthened that without good cause says 'no' to children?

? Are spouses likely to grow in marital harmony?

? Do they grow in marital unity?

? Could contraceptive usage affect their fidelity to each other?

? Is their marital love more fulfilled?

? Do they tend to grow closer together or move apart?

? Is Christ truly accepted as Lord and Master in their marriage and fertility?

? Is contraceptive use a private decision that affects only the persons using it?

Other works by Patrick McCrystal

✎ **What Kind of Prescription?**
A pharmacist addresses his professional peers on the ethical dilemma of dispensing abortifacient drugs.
An article that caused quite a stir in the pharmacy profession. *Chemist and Druggist* 25 February 1995

📖 **Contraception and *Evangelium Vitae* (1996)**
The author's first book exploring the abortifacient nature of contraceptive products in light of Pope John Paul II's encyclical *Evangelium Vitae.*
Published by Aras Mhuire Publications, 39 Mountjoy Square, Dublin 1
☎ Tel +353 1 855 2790

📷 **Abortifacient Contraceptives**
Audiotapes and DVD's of conference talks by the author.
Available from Human Life International (Ireland), 6 Belvedere Place, Dublin 1
☎ Tel +353 1 855 2504

✎ **Sexual Health or Contraceptive Evangelism?**
A pharmacist questions his profession's promotion of condoms and the so-called 'morning-after' pill. *Northern Ireland Pharmacy in Focus*, Issue 37, January 2007
Can be downloaded from www.hliireland.ie or www.dangersofcontraception.com

📄 **The Glorious Pill? Why You Should Not Use Contraception.**
Leaflet with extensive references, 2009. Download from www.hliireland.ie or www.dangersofcontraception.com